◌ human rights *first*

U.S. Detention of Asylum Seekers

Seeking Protection, Finding Prison

2009

About Human Rights First

Human Rights First believes that building respect for human rights and the rule of law will help ensure the dignity to which every individual is entitled and will stem tyranny, extremism, intolerance, and violence.

Human Rights First protects people at risk: refugees who flee persecution, victims of crimes against humanity or other mass human rights violations, victims of discrimination, those whose rights are eroded in the name of national security, and human rights advocates who are targeted for defending the rights of others. These groups are often the first victims of societal instability and breakdown; their treatment is a harbinger of wider-scale repression. Human Rights First works to prevent violations against these groups and to seek justice and accountability for violations against them.

Human Rights First is practical and effective. We advocate for change at the highest levels of national and international policymaking. We seek justice through the courts. We raise awareness and understanding through the media. We build coalitions among those with divergent views. And we mobilize people to act.

Human Rights First is a nonprofit, nonpartisan international human rights organization based in New York and Washington D.C. To maintain our independence, we accept no government funding.

This report is available for free online at www.humanrightsfirst.org

© 2009 Human Rights First. All Rights Reserved.

April 2009 – Revised June 2009

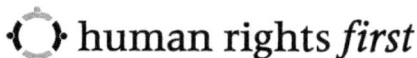

Acknowledgements

The principal authors of this report were Eleanor Acer and Jessica Chicco, and Ms. Chicco was the primary researcher. Additional research, writing and/or editing was contributed by Elizabeth Centeno, Anwen Hughes, Asa Piyaka, Anne Sovcik, and Tad Stahnke. We thank Sarah Graham for her work designing the report, and Brett Deutsch for contributing his photographs.

We wish to thank the many rsefugees and asylum seekers, pro bono attorneys, legal representation organizations, faith-based and community groups, Department of Homeland Security and Department of Justice officials, and others who provided information included in this report.

Human Rights First gratefully acknowledges the Fund for New Jersey, the Fund for New Citizens of the New York Community Trust, and the Picower Foundation for their generous support of our pro bono legal representation program for refugees who seek asylum in the United States.

{ } human rights *first*

Headquarters

333 Seventh Avenue
13th Floor
New York, NY 10001-5108

Tel.: 212.845.5200
Fax: 212.845.5299

Washington D.C. Office

100 Maryland Avenue, NE
Suite 500
Washington, DC 20002-5625

Tel: 202.547.5692
Fax: 202.543.5999

www.humanrightsfirst.org

Table of Contents

Executive Summary

"When I was back home I was in prison [for speaking out for human rights]. I thought that when I got to America I'd be free, but then I was in prison again. I was surprised by that."

Burmese school teacher who was beaten and jailed for two years by the Burmese government, and then detained by U.S. immigration authorities for seven months in an El Paso, Texas, immigration jail after requesting asylum in the United States[1]

IN MARCH 2003, the U.S. Department of Homeland Security (DHS) took over responsibility for asylum and immigration matters when the former INS (Immigration and Naturalization Service) was abolished. With this transfer, DHS was entrusted with the duty to ensure that the United States lives up to its commitments to those who seek asylum from persecution. These commitments stem from both U.S. law and international treaties with which the United States has pledged to abide. Yet, those who seek asylum—a form of protection extended to victims of political, religious and other forms of persecution—have been swept up in a wave of increased immigration detention, which has left many asylum seekers in jails and jail-like facilities for months or even years.

Six years after DHS and its interior immigration enforcement component, U.S. Immigration and Customs Enforcement (known as "ICE") took over responsibility for immigration detention, the U.S. system for detaining asylum seekers is more flawed than ever. As detailed in this report, thousands of asylum seekers have been detained during these years. In 2007 alone, more than 10,000 asylum seekers were newly detained in the United States. They are held in facilities that are actual jails or are operated like jails. They are often brought in handcuffs and sometimes shackles to these facilities, where they wear

prison uniforms, are guarded by officers in prison attire, visit with family and friends only through glass barriers, and have essentially no freedom of movement within the facilities. The cost of detaining these asylum seekers over the past six years has exceeded $300 million.[2] During that time, ICE parole policies have become more restrictive, and parole rates for asylum seekers dropped from 41.3 percent in 2004 to 4.2 percent in 2007. ICE has not provided Congressionally-mandated statistics—detailing the number of asylum seekers detained, the length of their detention, and the rates of their release—in a timely or complete manner. The U.S. detention system for asylum seekers, which lacks crucial safeguards, is inconsistent with international refugee protection and human rights standards.

DHS and ICE have increased their use of prison-like facilities by at least 62 percent—with six new mega-facilities added in just the last five years.[3] Some of these facilities are located far from legal representation and the immigration courts. More than a third of detained asylum seekers are not represented by legal counsel, even though asylum seekers are much more likely to be granted asylum in immigration court when they are represented.[4] At these remote facilities, detained asylum seekers often see U.S. immigration judges and asylum officers only on television sets, with immigration court asylum hearings and asylum office "credible fear" interviews (which determine whether an individual will even be allowed to apply for asylum or will instead be summarily deported) increasingly conducted by video. In fact, more than 60 percent of credible fear interviews were conducted by video in 2007. A recent study demonstrated that asylum seekers who have their immigration court asylum hearings conducted by video are about half as likely to be granted asylum.[5]

Through our *pro bono* representation work, and in conducting research for this report, we have learned of many refugees who were jailed for many months—and some for years—in these prison-like facilities before being granted asylum in this country. Many asylum seekers could have been released from detention while their cases were pending, either on parole or through an immigration court custody hearing. Providing asylum seekers with access to fair release procedures does not undermine security. In fact, the Department of Homeland Security's regulations and guidelines on parole expressly prohibit the release of an individual who presents a risk to the community or a flight or security risk. The case law governing immigration court custody hearings also requires that the individual establish that he or she does not present a danger to others, a threat to national security, or a flight risk.[6]

In some cases, asylum seekers could have been released, at significant savings, to a supervised release program. In fact, while detention costs $95 each day on average, alternatives to detention cost $10 to $14 for each person each day. Individuals who have been released through these programs have continued to appear for their immigration court hearings at high rates—ranging from 93 to 99 percent. According to ICE, participants in the intensive supervision appearance program (ISAP) demonstrated a 91 percent compliance with removal orders as well.[7]

Here are just a few examples of some of the refugees who have been detained for months or years in jails or jail-like facilities in this country:[8]

■ A Guinean human rights activist, who had been abducted by government security forces in his country, was detained for four and a half months in a U.S. immigration jail in New Jersey. He was only released three weeks before being granted asylum by a U.S. immigration court.

■ A Baptist Chin woman from Burma was detained in an El Paso, Texas, immigration jail for over two years. ICE denied several parole requests even though she had proof of her identity and family in the U.S.—only paroling her after 25 months in detention. She was subsequently granted asylum in 2008.

■ An Afghan teacher who was threatened by the Taliban spent 20 months in detention at three county jails in Illinois and Wisconsin. The teacher was denied release on parole by ICE despite having letters of support from U.S. government officials who knew him because he taught at an educational institution sponsored by U.S. and NATO forces in Afghanistan. After a U.S. federal court found him eligible for asylum, he was finally released from detention on an electronic monitoring bracelet until a final decision granting asylum was made by the immigration judge in early 2009.

■ A Tibetan man, who was detained for more than a year and tortured by Chinese authorities after putting up pro-Tibetan independence posters, was detained for 11 months at the Elizabeth Detention Center in New Jersey before being granted asylum by a U.S. immigration court.

In examining the U.S. detention system and in providing *pro bono* legal assistance to individual asylum seekers, Human Rights First has interviewed scores of refugees who have been detained in the United States in recent years before being granted asylum by U.S. authorities. We have also visited over ten immigration jails and detention centers in New Jersey, New York, South Carolina, Texas, and Virginia (and were denied access to facilities in California and Illinois), met with local and national immigration officials, reviewed government reports, sought statistics and documents through a series of Freedom of Information Act requests, and interviewed faith-based and other legal providers, clergy and community service groups.[9] Our recommendations, outlined at the end of this report, do not undermine this country's security. The United States can both maintain its security while also living up to its commitments to those who seek protection from persecution.

Increase in Prison-Like Facilities

> *"I didn't expect to be in jail for six months. I'm not a criminal. I didn't expect to be transported in chains. This is not what I imagined. Especially not from America."*
>
> Refugee from Ethiopia, detained in a Virginia county jail by ICE for six months during 2007 and 2008 before being granted asylum

Since 2002, the number of immigrants detained each year has more than doubled—with an increase from 202,000 in 2002 to an estimated population of 442,941 in 2009. Between 2005 and 2008 alone, ICE increased detention beds by 78 percent.[10] While the vast majority of immigration detainees are not asylum seekers, well over 48,000 asylum seekers have been detained in U.S. jails and immigration detention centers from 2003 to 2009. While Congress required U.S. immigration authorities to provide

data relating to the detention and parole of asylum seekers, ICE has not provided complete statistical information for these years, and no records for 2005 or 2008 in response to Human Rights First's requests under the Freedom of Information Act. As a result, we do not know the exact number of asylum seekers detained during this time—only that it certainly exceeds 48,000.[11]

Between 2003 and 2009, DHS and ICE oversaw:

- An increase of at least 62 percent in the use of prison-like detention for asylum seekers and other immigrants—from 20,662 beds in 2002 to 33,400 beds in jails and jail-like facilities in 2009.[12]

- Treatment of asylum seekers like prisoners in correctional facilities in these jails and jail-like facilities. They are often handcuffed and sometimes shackled when transported, required to wear prison-like uniforms—even when they appear in immigration court in front of a judge—and only allowed to visit with family and friends through a glass partition.

- The opening of a "family" detention facility—housed in a former medium-security prison—to detain 500 asylum seekers, other immigrants, and their families. Children and their parents were all required to wear prison uniforms, until a lawsuit settlement in August 2007 changed this.

- The opening of at least six new mega-detention facilities holding more than 1,000 immigration detainees each, for a total of nearly 10,000 beds.

Facility	Detention Beds
Northwest Detention Center (Wash., 2004)	1,061
South Texas Detention Center (Tex., 2005)	1,904
Willacy Detention Center (Tex., 2006)	3,000
Stewart Detention Center (Ga., 2006)	1,524
Jena Detention Center (La., 2007)	1,162
Otero County Processing Center (N.M., 2008)	1,088
TOTAL	**9,739**

Human Rights First staff, accompanied by *pro bono* attorneys and representatives of local faith and community groups, visited two of these facilities, including the South Texas Detention Center—a 1,904-bed facility located 57 miles south of San Antonio on the outskirts of the small town of Pearsall. The detention center is surrounded by high barbed wire fences, and looks and feels like a prison. Asylum seekers and other detainees are required to wear prison-like uniforms and are held nearly 24 hours a day in "pods"—large rooms where as many as 100 asylum seekers and immigrant detainees sleep on narrow bunk beds, eat their meals, and use the showers and toilets, which are located behind only a short wall. Asylum seekers held at this facility have come from a number of countries including Burma, China, Colombia, Eritrea, Ethiopia, Honduras, Iraq, and Somalia. More than 2,700 asylum seekers were detained at the facility during 2007 alone.[13]

"[C]ontrary to USCIRF recommendations, DHS's use of jails and jail-like facilities has increased in the past few years."

U.S. Commission on International Religious Freedom letter to DHS Assistant Secretary for Policy Stewart Baker, January 8, 2009[14]

In a comprehensive 500-page study authorized by Congress and issued in February 2005, the bipartisan governmental U.S. Commission on International Religious Freedom (USCIRF) concluded that it was not appropriate for the United States to detain asylum seekers in prison-like conditions. The Commission recommended that the criteria for release of asylum seekers on parole be put into regulations, and that when detention was necessary, ICE should use less restrictive (yet secure) facilities. Guidelines issued by the United Nations High Commissioner for Refugees (UNHCR) have also made clear that, when asylum seekers are detained, "[t]he use of prisons should be avoided."[15]

Instead of decreasing its reliance on jails and jail-like detention, the Department of Homeland Security has actually *increased* its use of these facilities—adding or using, according to Human Rights First's calculations, more than 9,000 additional immigration detention beds in jails or jail-like facilities since the Commission issued its report in February 2005.[16]

Deficient Medical Care in Detention

U.S. government assessments and media reports have found serious deficiencies in the health care provided to asylum seekers and immigrants in U.S. immigration detention, including:

■ Severe staffing shortages, with nearly 140 medical staff openings and an 18 percent vacancy rate for medical staff;

■ 90 deaths of detainees since ICE's inception in 2003, including 13 suicides; and

■ Failure to use interpreters to communicate with detainees during medical exams, in some cases leading to dangerous misdiagnoses.[17]

For example, a refugee from Somalia was misdiagnosed and given anti-psychotic drugs by the doctor who examined her at an immigration detention center in Elizabeth, New Jersey. Her *pro bono* attorney, recruited by Human Rights First, repeatedly contacted the facility to express concern after two outside doctors reported that she appeared "dull, or drugged," began lactating, and suffered from nausea and vomiting.[18]

Detention Without Safeguards

"Parole is available for Mother Teresa."

ICE detention and removal officer at an Arizona facility, early 2008[19]

The current system for detaining asylum seekers who request protection at U.S. airports and borders is inconsistent with international standards.[20] Asylum seekers have been detained for months or sometimes for years, even when they can establish their identities, community ties, and that they do not present a flight risk or a danger to the community. The initial detention is "mandatory" under the expedited removal provisions of the 1996 immigration laws. The decision to release an asylum seeker on parole—or to continue his or her detention for longer—is entrusted to local officials with ICE, which is the detaining authority, rather than to an independent authority or court. The parole criteria that are specific to asylum seekers are contained in an ICE policy directive rather than the relevant regulations and have often been ignored by local officials who may base their decisions on other factors, such as the availability of "bed space" at local facilities. The system also fails to provide for regular review of the need for continued detention although an asylum seeker's case may take months or even years to make its way through the adjudication system.[21]

ICE acts, in effect, as both judge and jailer with respect to parole decisions for asylum seekers. If parole is denied by ICE, the decision cannot be appealed to a judge—even an immigration judge. While immigration judges can review ICE custody decisions for other immigration detainees, they are precluded under regulatory language from reviewing the detention of so-called "arriving aliens," a group that consists overwhelmingly of the asylum seekers who are detained when they seek protection upon arriving at airports and other U.S. entry points.[22]

In the years since DHS and ICE took over responsibility for the detention of asylum seekers:

- The rate of release on parole for asylum seekers appears to have dropped. Statistics provided to Human Rights First by ICE indicate that the rate at which asylum seekers who have passed their screening interviews are being released on parole has dropped sharply—from 66.6 percent in 2004 to 4.5 percent in 2007.[23]

- ICE issued a more restrictive parole policy for asylum seekers—a policy that is inconsistent with the recommendations of the U.S. Commission on International Religious Freedom. The new policy, issued in November 2007, includes an additional set of assessments, and does not require ICE to determine the eligibility of all detained asylum seekers for parole. As a result, asylum seekers who are not represented or who do not speak or write English may not be assessed for release on parole.[24]

- In interviews with Human Rights First researchers, attorneys who work with asylum seekers across the country reported that parole remains difficult to obtain for the asylum seekers whom they believe meet the criteria. In one location, Human Rights First has observed an increased parole rate, though the change may be due to staff changes at the local ICE office.

- In several locations, asylum seekers have been required to post bonds that are simply too high for this population to be able to pay—resulting in many months of additional detention for some asylum seekers.

- While the use of various supervised release and electronic monitoring programs have increased—primarily as the result of some specific congressional funding—ICE has not implemented an effective nationwide program of "alternatives to detention."

- Asylum seekers are detained on average at least three months (though this average does not take into account longer term detentions across fiscal years), and many are detained for longer. Asylum seekers are held on average longer than most immigration detainees. [25]

As a result, many asylum seekers who could have been released from detention have been jailed by ICE in U.S. jails and immigration detention centers for months or longer. Here are just a few examples:[26]

- **Tibetan monk detained in Texas for over a year.** A Tibetan monk, who supported the Dalai Lama and was arrested for participating in pro-Tibetan demonstrations, was detained at an immigration jail in south Texas while his request for asylum was pending. He remained in detention for more than a year even though his attorney had previously made a request to ICE for his release on parole, and he had proof of his identity as well as a sponsor willing to house him. He was only released from detention after the U.S. immigration court granted his request for asylum.

- **Pastor from Liberia detained in New Jersey immigration jail.** A Pentecostal pastor who fled Liberia, after learning he was in danger because he criticized the use of child soldiers by the forces of Charles Taylor, was detained for three and a half months in a New Jersey immigration jail. His request for release on parole, which was supported by religious leaders in West Virginia, Virginia, and Maryland, was denied by ICE. He was only released from detention after he was granted asylum by a U.S. immigration court.

- **Colombian refugee detained in Arizona immigration jail for over a year.** A Colombian refugee, who had been detained and tortured following his participation in a political demonstration in Colombia, was detained in a U.S. immigration jail in Arizona for 14 months even though he could have been released to the care of his U.S. citizen father and daughter. ICE denied his request for release on parole, even after an immigration court had ruled he was eligible for asylum. This refugee was finally released from detention two weeks after the judge's ruling was affirmed on appeal.

A pastor from Liberia was detained for three and a half months in a New Jersey immigration jail. He was denied parole and was only released after a U.S. immigration court granted him asylum.

Impact of Detention on Asylum Seekers

"I was scared. I thought they might beat me, because when I was in Tibet the Chinese beat me all the time."

Refugee from Tibet, who was in immigration detention in the United States for 11 months before being granted asylum by a U.S. immigration court.

Over the last six years, medical and mental health experts have documented the harmful impact of detention on the physical and mental health of asylum seekers. One report, issued by Physicians for Human Rights (PHR) and the Bellevue/NYU Program for Survivors of Torture, concluded that detention inflicts further harm on what is an already traumatized population. The report found that detained asylum seekers suffer from extremely high levels of anxiety, depression, and Post Traumatic Stress Disorder (PTSD), and that their psychological health worsens the longer they remain in custody. In fact, uncertainty about the length of detention was itself a significant cause of anxiety and mental distress. [27]

Detention also impacts the ability of an asylum seeker to establish his or her eligibility for asylum. Not only is it more difficult for a detained asylum seeker to gather documentation in support of his or her case, but it is also more difficult for that asylum seeker to secure legal representation. (Unlike in the criminal justice system, the civil immigration system does not provide attorneys for individuals who are unable to afford private counsel.) U.S. government statistics confirm that representation rates are much lower for asylum seekers who are detained in this country: more than a third of detained asylum seekers do not have legal representation. At the same time, multiple studies, based on government statistics, have confirmed that asylum seekers who are represented are three times as likely to be granted asylum.

Some asylum seekers abandon their requests for asylum in the United States, because they cannot bear to be detained any longer in a U.S. immigration jail. Others give up efforts to block their deportation while their cases are on appeal. For example, after over 17 months in a U.S. immigration detention facility and a local jail, a young woman from Colombia decided to accept deportation because she could no longer cope with the stress of detention. A U.S. Court of Appeals subsequently ruled that she had a well-founded fear of persecution in Colombia. The court noted that the asylum seeker had "averred that despite the fact that her 'fear of persecution is as strong as ever[,]' the detention was, in her words, 'affecting me physically and destroying me mentally' and suggested that her detention in the United States served as a daily and unwelcome reminder of the indignity of detention at the hands of the FARC [an armed guerilla group that had abducted her twice]."[28]

Financial Cost of Detention

The financial cost of immigration detention has skyrocketed in recent years, with ICE's detention and removal budget doubling in the past four years. In 2009, ICE will be paying $1.7 billion for "custody operations." Releasing eligible asylum seekers on parole, or to a "supervised release" program, is much more cost effective. While detention averages $95 per day, alternatives to detention range from $10 to $14 a day; and release through regular parole incurs no additional daily cost.[29] ICE does not report on the amount it spends to detain asylum seekers, who constitute only a portion of detained immigrants—and indeed does not precisely track the number of detained asylum seekers or the actual length of their detention. Using various government statistics, Human Rights First has calculated that ICE spent somewhere over $300 million to detain asylum seekers from 2003 to February 2009. The costs are likely higher as ICE has not provided to Human Rights First statistics for 2005 or 2008, and ICE does not include longer term detentions in the averages it has provided.[30]

While costs at different facilities vary, Human Rights First has calculated that:

- ICE spent more than $12 million to detain over 2,000 asylum seekers at the South Texas Detention Center in Pearsall during 2007;

- ICE spent about $90,000 to detain a refugee woman from Burma in an El Paso, Texas immigration jail for over two years;

- ICE spent nearly $115,000 to detain an asylum seeker from Sri Lanka at the Elizabeth, New Jersey detention facility for two and a half years, before releasing him on an electronic monitoring device; and

- ICE spent more than $15,000 to detain a refugee from Zimbabwe for three months, more than $20,000 to detain a refugee from Haiti for four months—both in New Jersey—and nearly $20,000 to detain a Tibetan refugee for eight months in California.[31]

Escalation of Detention in Remote Areas

The 3,000-bed Willacy Detention Center in Raymondville, Texas—nicknamed "Tent City" and "Ritmo"—opened in 2006.

As DHS and ICE have expanded immigration detention over the last few years, they have repeatedly chosen to detain asylum seekers and immigrants in new facilities that are located in areas that are not near *pro bono* legal resources, the immigration courts, and U.S. asylum offices. In too many instances, facilities used by ICE were opened or used for months or even years before a Legal Orientation Program was put in place to provide basic legal information to detainees—a decision which left thousands of asylum seekers and other immigrant detainees without basic legal information and counseling to help them navigate the system and try to obtain legal representation. The remote location of some of these facilities has also made it much more difficult for many of these asylum seekers to secure legal representation.

At the same time, asylum seekers and other immigrant detainees increasingly see immigration judges and U.S. asylum officers not in person but only on television screens—with video conferencing equipment being installed in 47 immigration courts and more than 77 other locations, including detention centers. For example, the new facility in Pearsall, Texas—where more than 2,700 "credible fear" asylum seekers were held in 2007—the Willacy Detention Center in Raymondville, Texas, and the Otay Mesa Facility in San Diego, California are all outfitted with video conferencing equipment. At these facilities, nearly all immigration court hearings are conducted by video. Asylum seekers who have their asylum hearings conducted by video are about half as likely to be granted asylum according to a 2008 study based on immigration court statistics, which was published in the Georgetown Immigration Law Journal.[32] A finding by the immigration court as to the asylum seeker's credibility is central to the claim. However, the study concludes that the use of video conferencing alters the way a judge perceives an asylum applicant's testimony and the technology does not accurately capture and convey non-verbal elements, some changes in tone, and body language. The U.S. asylum office, a division of the U.S. Citizenship and Immigration Services, conducted over 60 percent of "credible fear" screening interviews by video conference in 2007, primarily through its Houston office. According to statistics provided by the asylum office, the "pass" rates for credible fear interviews conducted in-person and those conducted by video conference are comparable. Statistics also show a substantial drop in credible fear pass rates between 2004 and 2008.[33]

Looking Forward

The United States has pledged to treat those who seek asylum in this country in accordance with its commitments under the Refugee Convention and its Protocol, and the International Covenant on Civil and Political Rights, which protects individuals from arbitrary detention. Under international standards, asylum seekers should generally not be detained. When they are, that detention should have adequate safeguards, including procedures to ensure review by an independent authority or court. When some supervision is necessary, alternatives to detention should be used. And when an asylum seeker is detained, he or she should not be held in penal or prison-like conditions.

As the new leadership of the Department of Homeland Security reviews policies, practices, and structures, it has the opportunity to reform detention policies and practices—and to ensure that the Department adequately prioritizes the protection of those who flee to this country in search of refuge. The Secretary of Homeland Security should direct the Department of Homeland Security, Immigration and Customs Enforcement, U.S. Citizenship and Immigration Services, and Customs and Border Protection to implement the reforms outlined in this report. In making some of these changes, the Department of Homeland Security and the Department of Justice will need to work together. The new leadership of the Department of Justice should review and revise the Department's regulations, policies, and practices to ensure that the U.S. meets its commitments to refugees and asylum seekers under both U.S. and international law.

In addition to providing crucial oversight, Congress should also take steps to ensure lasting reforms by passing legislation that puts critical safeguards on the use of detention into law.

A more detailed set of recommendations is included at the end of this report. Outlined below are some critical first steps:

1. Review of Detention by the Immigration Courts

The Departments of Justice and Homeland Security should revise current regulatory language to provide arriving asylum seekers with the chance to have their custody reviewed in a hearing before an immigration court, a safeguard afforded other immigration detainees.[34] In revising these provisions, the regulations should make clear that any bond requirements should be appropriate to the circumstances and means of the asylum seeker, and that the immigration courts can direct that an individual be released into an alternatives to detention program.

The U.S. Congress should also enact legislation providing these asylum seekers with access to immigration court custody hearings to ensure lasting change by putting this change into law as well.

2. Other Reforms to Limit Unnecessary Detention

In addition to ensuring immigration court review of detention for asylum seekers, the **Department of Homeland Security and Immigration and Customs Enforcement** should reform the parole process and create a nationwide program for supervised release or other alternatives to detention.

■ **Reform the Parole Process.** The Department of Homeland Security, Immigration and Customs Enforcement, should issue regulations providing for the release of an asylum seeker who can establish identity, has ties to the community, satisfies the credible fear standard, and does not pose a danger to the community. Asylum seekers who are determined by

immigration courts to be entitled to asylum or withholding of removal should be released.

■ **Create a Nationwide System of Supervised Release.** When an asylum seeker is not eligible for release on parole and some additional supervision is determined to be necessary, the individual should be assessed for release to a supervised release program or other alternative-to-detention program. These programs should include community support mechanisms, such as case managers, referrals to legal and social service providers, and assistance accessing information relating to immigration proceedings. Electronic monitoring devices (ankle bracelets) should only be used when determined to be necessary after a fair and individualized assessment, and should not be used in a manner that restricts freedom of movement to such an extent as to essentially constitute continued custody.

3. Stop Using Jail-like Facilities

The Department of Homeland Security and Immigration and Customs Enforcement should stop using jails and jail-like facilities to detain asylum seekers and other immigration detainees. The Department should also end the practice of detaining families. Instead, asylum seekers should be:

■ Released from detention on parole or through an immigration court custody hearing if they meet the applicable criteria; or

■ Released to a supervised release program, or other alternative to detention program, if some supervision of the release is necessary.

When asylum seekers are detained—during the period of initial "mandatory" detention under the U.S. expedited removal statute, or if continued detention is determined to be necessary after a fair and individualized assessment—they should not be held in penal or prison-like facilities, but rather in facilities where they can wear their own clothing and the conditions of their detention are not prison-like, as outlined below.

4. Stop Opening Remote Facilities and Ensure Adequate Legal and Other Support *Prior* to Using Facilities

The **Department of Homeland Security and Immigration and Customs Enforcement** should stop opening and using facilities located in remote areas that are far from legal representation resources, immigration courts, or an adequate pool of medical staff.

The **Department of Homeland Security and Immigration and Customs Enforcement** should work with the **Department of Justice** and **U.S. Citizenship and Immigration Services** to ensure that legal orientation presentations, access to adequate legal representation, full medical staffing, immigration judges and asylum officers (in-person, and not by video conferencing), and pastoral care are actually in place and funded *before* detaining asylum seekers or other immigrants at a facility.

Both the **immigration courts** and the **U.S. Citizenship and Immigration Services asylum office** should devote adequate staffing to—and **Congress** should provide adequate funding to—conduct asylum hearings and credible fear interviews in person and in a timely manner. ICE should not open and use facilities in areas that will not be accessible for immigration judges and asylum officers. The immigration courts should stop conducting asylum merit hearings by video.

5. Improve the Conditions of Detention

Detention Should Not Be Based on a Penal Model. The detention standards should be revised to provide for detention in which individuals can, for example: wear their own clothing (rather than prison uniforms); have contact visitation (as opposed to visits through plexi-glass barriers)

with family and friends; and have freedom of movement within the secure facility (so they can use outdoor areas, libraries, indoor recreation, or cafeteria areas during the course of the day). Officers should not wear prison guard uniforms, but should be dressed in an alternate uniform, such as a white shirt and tan pants. Handcuffs and shackles should not be used in facilities or during transportation absent extraordinary circumstances. Some of these changes could, and should, be made at some facilities immediately.

Medical and Mental Health Care Must be Improved. The Department of Homeland Security and ICE should take steps to improve the provision of medical and mental health care at all facilities where asylum seekers and other immigrant detainees are held, seeking input from independent experts and medical professionals, many of whom have provided detailed recommendations on improving medical care.[35] These reforms should ensure that:

- Medical units have an appropriate level of staffing *prior* to detaining asylum seekers and other immigrants at a facility, and a mechanism to ensure that detainees are removed from facilities that do not have adequate medical staffing.

- Interpretation services are appropriately used during medical visits at all facilities, including by creating a mechanism and/or form to evaluate and monitor the use of interpreters by medical staff at facilities.

- Mental health care should include specialized counseling for survivors of torture and trauma.

Congress should continue to provide increased oversight on issues relating to detainee health care and deaths, and should pass legislation mandating improved medical care and the independent investigation of detainee deaths.

6. Protection Mechanisms at the Department of Homeland Security

The **Secretary of Homeland Security** should:

- **Create an Asylum and Refugee Protection Office within the DHS Secretary's Office.** This office should ensure that policies, practices and legal interpretations relating to asylum seekers and refugees are consistent with this country's legal commitments and that the reforms recommended in this report are implemented. This office, as detailed in the recommendations at the end of this report, should be provided with the resources, staffing and authority to oversee policies and practices relating to asylum seekers and refugees throughout DHS.

- **Maintain a Senior Refugee and Asylum Policy position** in the DHS policy office, and provide sufficient staffing and resources.

- **Strengthen the Deputy Secretary's** capacity and chain-of-command authority to ensure that the Asylum and Refugee Protection Office's directives and guidance are followed by the various immigration-related agencies.

- **Direct the DHS General Counsel** to make asylum seeker and refugee protection a priority.

7. Provide Timely and Accurate Statistics

The **Department of Homeland Security** should ensure that **Immigration and Customs Enforcement** improves its systems for tracking data relating to the detention of asylum seekers, including data reflecting the number of detained asylum seekers, their age, their gender, the location of their detention, the length of their detention, and their parole or release from detention. This information, which is required by law to be provided annually to Congress and to the public on request, should be provided to both Congress and the public immediately after the end of each fiscal year in a timely manner.

8. Improve Conduct of Expedited Removal

The **Department of Homeland Security** should ensure that **U.S. Customs and Border Protection (CBP)** implements critical reforms recommended by the U.S. Commission on International Religious Freedom, ensures that procedures designed to protect asylum seekers from being returned to persecution are followed, and stops detaining asylum seekers who arrive with valid visas that are considered invalid by CBP solely because the individual requests asylum.

U.S. Citizenship and Immigration Services should request and allocate appropriate funding so that credible fear interviews are conducted in person and in a timely manner; and conduct an assessment of the decline in the credible fear grant rate, the decline in referrals for credible fear interviews and the impact of video conferencing on the conduct and outcomes of credible fear interviews.

Congress should authorize the U.S. Commission on International Religious Freedom to conduct a review of the expanded use of expedited removal and its impact on asylum seekers, and should provide appropriate funding for this assessment.

Introduction and Background

"To hear that America is a country of freedom, and you decided to ask for protection, and then you're put in jail, I was very surprised...This was my first experience going to jail. I had never broken the law before."

Refugee from Cameroon who was detained for nearly 11 months in county jails in Illinois and Wisconsin and denied release on parole. He was granted asylum in September 2008.

U.S. Tradition of Welcoming the Persecuted

n the wake of World War II, the United States played a leading role in building an international refugee protection regime to ensure that the world's nations would never again refuse to extend shelter to refugees fleeing persecution and harm. The United States has committed to the central guarantees of the 1951 Refugee Convention and its 1967 Protocol. The United States passed the Refugee Act of 1980 in order to bring the country's laws into compliance with the Refugee Convention and Protocol, by incorporating into U.S. law the Convention's definition of a "refugee" and the principle of *non-refoulement*—which prohibits the return of refugees to countries where they would face persecution. [36]

In 2008, 10,000 refugees were granted asylum by U.S. asylum officers, and nearly 11,000 more were granted asylum by U.S. immigration courts. [37] In addition to providing protection to asylum seekers who have already reached its shores, the United States has also played a leading role in the resettlement of refugees who are stranded in refugee camps and other locations abroad. This country has brought nearly 2.8 million refugees to safety here in the last thirty years, and the U.S. resettlement program serves as a model to the rest of the world. [38]

The Department of Homeland Security and Asylum Seekers

On March 1, 2003, the Immigration and Naturalization Service (INS) was abolished and its functions transferred to the new Department of Homeland Security (DHS). The mission of DHS, which is spelled out in the Homeland Security Act, is to prevent terrorist attacks in the United States, reduce the vulnerability of the United States to terrorism, and minimize the damage from terrorist attacks. [39] As a result of this transfer of immigration functions, asylum seekers now interact with three separate bureaus within DHS:

■ When an asylum seeker arrives at an airport or a border entry post, he or she is initially inspected and interviewed by officers from **U.S. Customs and Border Protection (CBP)**. If encountered in the border areas, asylum seekers are detained and interviewed by officers with the Border Patrol, also part of CBP.

- If that asylum seeker is detained, **U.S. Immigration and Customs Enforcement (ICE)** is the component agency responsible for his or her detention. ICE "trial attorneys" will also represent the agency in immigration court removal proceedings, typically opposing the asylum seeker's request for protection.

- Before the asylum seeker will even be allowed to request asylum, though, he or she will first have to be interviewed by an asylum officer with **U.S. Citizenship and Immigration Services (USCIS)**. USCIS also conducts asylum interviews for asylum seekers who apply for protection after they have entered the country and who are not generally detained.

This separation of immigration functions, coupled with the Department's mission, raised concerns from the start that cross-cutting issues relating to the protection of asylum seekers and refugees would "fall between the cracks" or be difficult to resolve within DHS. As a result, Human Rights First recommended that the Department create a high-level office to coordinate and ensure protection for refugees and asylum seekers.[40] In its 2005 report, the U.S. Commission on International Religious Freedom (USCIRF) found that it was "exceedingly difficult to address inter-bureau issues" relating to the detention of asylum seekers and expedited removal, and recommended that DHS create an office to coordinate policy and monitor the implementation of procedures affecting refugees and asylum seekers.[41]

While former DHS Secretary Michael Chertoff created a new position of Special Advisor for Refugee and Asylum Affairs in 2006, the office was quickly given broader responsibility over immigration policy, limiting its capacity to address and resolve a range of cross-cutting refugee issues, including the detention of asylum seekers. In fact, it took the Department nearly four years to issue a coordinated substantive response to the findings and recommendations of the U.S. Commission on International Religious Freedom's 2005 report.

Expedited Removal and Its Expansion

Since taking over immigration functions in 2003, the Department of Homeland Security has expanded its use of "expedited removal," a summary deportation process enacted in 1996 that provides for the "mandatory detention" of asylum seekers who are subject to its provisions. Under this expedited process, immigration officers were given the power to order the immediate deportation of people who arrive in the United States without proper travel documents—a power previously entrusted to immigration judges. Many refugees arrive without proper travel documents, unable to obtain them from the governments which they flee.

While genuine asylum seekers are not supposed to be deported under expedited removal, the process is so hasty and lacking in safeguards that mistakes can and do happen. In fact, USCIRF found serious flaws in maintaining safeguards in the process, documenting that immigration inspectors failed to inform individuals that they could ask for protection if they feared returning to their countries (in about half the cases observed by USCIRF experts) and ordered the deportation of individuals who expressed a fear of return (in 15 percent of the observed cases).[42]

When the expedited removal process was first created, the former INS applied it only to those who sought admission at a U.S. airport or border entry point without valid documents. Now, expedited removal also applies to those encountered within 100 miles of U.S. borders if they have been in the country for less than 14 days. The number of individuals subject to this summary process has increased significantly—in 2002, 34,624 individuals were deported through expedited removal, but this number more than tripled to 106,200 in fiscal year 2007.[43]

Haitian Pastor Detained For Requesting Protection

In the fall of 2004, the 81-year-old Reverend Joseph Dantica arrived at the Miami International Airport from Haiti, traveling on his own valid passport and visa. He had been persecuted in Haiti after U.N. forces and Haitian police officers fired at armed gang members from the roof of his church. After he indicated to U.S. immigration inspectors that he wanted to seek temporary asylum in the United States, the Customs and Border Protection officers detained him, considering his visa invalid because he honestly indicated that he might need protection.[44]

He was put into the expedited removal process and detained. Reverend Dantica was brought to the Krome immigration detention facility in Miami, where he was given a prison uniform to wear. At the facility, his blood pressure medication was taken from him. After several days in detention, Reverend Dantica collapsed during his credible fear screening interview, which was held at the detention facility. A nurse from the Division of Immigration Health Services (DIHS)—which provides health services for immigration detainees—accused him of faking his illness. Reverend Dantica was handcuffed and transported to a hospital where he died the next day.[45]

Individuals who express a fear or concern about return are not supposed to be immediately deported. Instead they are subject to "mandatory detention" until they are determined to have a "credible fear of persecution" by a U.S. asylum officer (or an immigration judge in a subsequent review). Even those who arrive on valid passports and otherwise valid visas are considered to be subject to the expedited removal process by U.S. Customs and Border Protection officers if they express a fear of return.[46] Indeed, a number of the asylum seekers interviewed by Human Rights First arrived in this country on their own valid passports. Those who do not meet the credible fear standard are deported, and those who do meet the standard are allowed to request asylum in the United States—though, as detailed in this report, they often remain in U.S. immigration jails for months or longer.

Despite the increase in the number of individuals placed into expedited removal, the number of individuals identified as potential asylum seekers by U.S. Customs and Border Protection officers has dropped significantly. Nearly 10,000 individuals were referred by immigration inspectors for "credible fear" interviews in 2002 (and therefore sent to U.S. detention facilities for these screenings instead of being immediately deported).[47] In fiscal year 2007, however, only 5,285 individuals were referred for these asylum screening interviews. In fiscal year 2008, the number was similar at 5,290.[48] In addition, the rate at which U.S. Citizenship and Immigration Services asylum officers have found asylum seekers to meet the "credible fear" standard has also fallen sharply. From 2000 to 2004, the average passing rate of those referred for a credible fear interview was 93 percent as reported by the U.S. Commission on International Religious Freedom.[49] By fiscal year 2008, the pass rate had dropped to 59 percent.[50] In some parts of the country these pass rates are significantly lower than the national average.[51]

Detention of Asylum Seekers

Since October 1, 2003, the Department of Homeland Security has detained more than 23,000 asylum seekers under the expedited removal process.[52] These asylum seekers—over 6,000 in 2007 and 2008 alone—were mandatorily detained upon their arrival or in border areas shortly after arrival, and were subsequently determined to have a credible fear of persecution by U.S. asylum adjudicators. In addition to those who are subject to expedited removal, thousands more asylum seekers are detained once they are already in the United States.[53] While asylum seekers who apply for protection "affirmatively" after they have entered the country are not generally detained, their detention is on the rise as well.[54]

Congress has mandated that the government gather and publish statistics on the detention and release of asylum seekers.[55] While Immigration and Customs Enforcement has not provided all of the required statistics, based on those that have been provided, it appears that at least 48,000 asylum seekers have been detained since March 2003 (when DHS took over immigration enforcement responsibilities)—though the actual number is likely significantly higher.[56]

Asylum seekers who have been detained under expedited removal can request that ICE release them on parole after they have been determined to meet the credible fear standard—but those who are detained on arrival are not given access to immigration court custody hearings, a safeguard that is provided to other asylum seeker and immigrant detainees. The Department of Homeland Security's regulations and guidelines on parole expressly prohibit the release of an individual who presents a risk to the community or a security risk. The case law governing immigration court custody hearings also requires that the individual establish that he or she does not present a danger to others, a threat to national security, or a flight risk.[57]

As detailed in this report, many asylum seekers remain in detention while their asylum cases are pending. According to U.S. government statistics from 2007—the last year for which such data has been provided—asylum seekers are detained for an average of more than three months (though, as discussed below, this "average" does not include some longer term detentions).[58] A survey of Human Rights First clients detained between 2003 and 2008 reflects an average length of detention of five to six months for those who were determined by U.S. adjudicators to be "refugees" entitled to protection. Many will remain in detention longer—sometimes even years—while their cases are decided.

Increase in Prison-Like Facilities

"It was like being in a cage for the first time, all the time, 24/7. You start thinking, Why are they treating me this way?"

Refugee from Zimbabwe, who was persecuted due to his pro-democracy advocacy and was detained in a New Jersey detention facility for over three months before being granted asylum

"The overwhelming majority of asylum seekers referred for credible fear are detained—for weeks or months and occasionally years—in penal or penitentiary-like facilities."

U.S. Commission on International Religious Freedom, Report Card, February 2007[59]

In the United States, the Department of Homeland Security uses jails and jail-like facilities to detain asylum seekers and other immigrants held for administrative immigration violations. Immigration and Customs Enforcement (ICE), the DHS component agency that currently has authority over the detention of asylum seekers, holds asylum seekers in jail-like detention centers managed by ICE or by private contractors, as well as in hundreds of county jails.[60] In these penal and penitentiary-like facilities, asylum seekers are treated like prisoners in correctional facilities. For example, they are typically handcuffed and sometimes shackled when transported, required to wear prison-like uniforms—even when they appear in immigration court in front of a judge—and only allowed to visit with family and friends through a glass partition.[61]

Refugee from Zimbabwe, who was persecuted due to his pro-democracy advocacy, and was detained at a U.S. immigration detention facility for over three months before being granted asylum. [Photo by Brett Deutsch]

DHS and ICE have increased their use of jail-like detention for asylum seekers and other immigrants by 62 percent since taking over responsibility for immigration enforcement in 2003. In 2002, the former INS used 20,662 jail-like detention "beds." Over recent years, this number has increased significantly—to 33,400 immigration detention "beds" in 2009. According to a February 2009 report by the Government Accountability Office, the average daily population of detainees grew by about 40 percent from fiscal year 2003 through fiscal year 2007, with the most growth occurring since 2005.[62]

In many of the detention centers and jails, asylum seekers and other immigrant detainees have little or no privacy.

In recent years, ICE has contracted with a number of private companies to open a series of massive new prison-like facilities. These facilities, located in Georgia, Louisiana, Texas, and Washington State, hold more than 1,000 immigrant and asylum seeker detainees each, for a total of nearly 10,000 new detention beds. ICE also rents bed-space from more than 500 state and county facilities to house over half of all immigration detainees.[63] Over the last year, Human Rights First staff have interviewed detainees and former detainees held at a dozen different detention centers and county jails in California, Illinois, New Jersey, New York, Texas, Virginia, and Washington State, and visited more than ten of these jails and jail-like facilities in New Jersey, New York, South Carolina, Texas, and Virginia. ICE denied our staff access to several additional facilities in Illinois and California.

In its February 2005 report, the bipartisan U.S. Commission on International Religious Freedom (USCIRF) concluded that it was not appropriate to detain asylum seekers in prison-like conditions, recommending instead the use of less restrictive (yet secure) facilities when detention was necessary.[64] Despite these recommenda-

tions, as the Commission observed in January 2009, "contrary to USCIRF recommendations, DHS's use of jails and jail-like facilities has increased in the past few years."[65] In fact, since the Commission released its report in early 2005, DHS has added more than 9,000 immigration detention beds in jails or jail-like facilities.[66]

The Prison Model Used for Detention of Asylum Seekers

"Upon arriving in El Paso, I turned myself into immigration because I did not know where I was. I thought that by doing this, I was coming in legally, and that the Americans would help me...Then two officers came and handcuffed me and took me to a jail in El Paso."

Refugee from Burma, detained for seven months at the El Paso Service Processing Center in Texas

"If someone came to ask refuge in your country, you don't have to put them in a jail. You have to try to find a way to help him out, because he came all the way from his country, running away, he finally gets here for refuge, and then you put him in jail."

Refugee from Burundi, granted asylum by the U.S. immigration court after four and a half months at the Port Isabel Service Processing Center in Texas

"It is what it is, we run a jail."

Superintendent of a Virginia county jail detaining 250 to 300 immigration detainees, including asylum seekers[67]

"They have this mentality: because I am here, they think I'm a criminal."

Asylum seeker from Zimbabwe, detained at the Hampton Roads Regional Jail in Virginia

Asylum seekers are detained in jails and jail-like facilities in nearly every state, including Arizona, California, Florida, Georgia, Illinois, Maryland, Minnesota, New Jersey, New Mexico, New York, Washington State, Texas, Virginia, and Wisconsin.[68] In nearly all of these facilities, ICE detains asylum seekers in penal and penitentiary-like conditions: asylum seekers and other immigrant detainees are stripped of their own clothing and given prison uniforms, not allowed any contact visits with family or friends, and lack meaningful privacy and access to outdoor recreation. Their freedom of movement within the facilities is restricted, and they typically spend 23 hours a day in their "pods"—large dormitories or common areas that can hold up to 100 people.

Handcuffs and Shackles. Human Rights First staff have, over the years, interviewed hundreds of asylum seekers who have been handcuffed by U.S. immigration authorities and their contractors upon arrival at U.S. airports or border entry points, and whenever they are transported—including when they are taken to court for a hearing or to the hospital.[69] When they are handcuffed, sometimes their wrists are also secured to a "belly chain" around their waists. The USCIRF's expert on detention conditions found use of physical restraint in 18 of the 19 facilities he surveyed. USCIRF also reported that staff at the Tri-County Jail in Ullin, Illinois, used handcuffs, belly chains, and shackles when detainees were transported outside the facility.[70] Immigrant detainees at the 1,030-bed Northwest Detention Center in Tacoma, Washington, are also handcuffed and shackled when they are transported, according to a June 2008 report by the Seattle University School of Law International Human Rights Clinic and the organization OneAmerica.[71] Arriving asylum seekers are usually handcuffed and shackled at the John F. Kennedy

International Airport in New York and the Newark Liberty Airport in New Jersey.[72] Asylum seekers apprehended at the El Paso, Texas border entry point have also described being handcuffed. An asylum seeker who was detained at the Greyhound bus station in New Orleans also reported being handcuffed and shackled with a belly chain by immigration officers. Furthermore, asylum seekers, like other immigration detainees, are sometimes shackled when they are brought before a judge for their hearings. Local practitioners report that this is often the case at immigration courts located in Chicago, San Francisco, Minnesota, New Jersey, and New York.[73] Even the ICE Detention Standards—which are modeled on penal standards—recognize that use of physical restraints should be limited to situations when restraints are needed "to gain control of a dangerous detainee, under specified conditions."[74]

"I saw two guys come and they're holding chains. They handcuff me. I said, What's happening? They said, It's for your safety and ours too. They handcuffed me and put a chain around my waist and shackled my legs... They took me to a vehicle and drove me to Elizabeth [Detention Center]."

Refugee from Zimbabwe, detained at New York's JFK International Airport; held in immigration detention for three months before being granted asylum

"The following day, they put me in handcuffs and shackled my feet. I asked the... officer, What did I do wrong, why did they need to shackle me? He said that was the rule."

Refugee from Cameroon, detained at Chicago O'Hare airport and detained in Illinois and Wisconsin county jails for 11 months before being granted asylum

Prison Uniforms and "Counts." At these prison-like detention centers and immigration jails, officers take away the clothes worn by asylum seekers and other immigration detainees, and give them jail-like uniforms to wear. At 16 of the 19 detention facilities surveyed by the Commission, asylum seekers were required to wear uniforms rather than their personal clothing.[75] A 2003 report by Physicians for Human Rights and the Bellevue/NYU Center for Survivors of Torture recommended that detained asylum seekers be permitted to wear their own clothing as a "simple, yet important" way for asylum seekers to be "able to identify themselves as individuals and not as criminals."[76] At these facilities, officers also conduct numerous detainee "counts" throughout the day, during which detainees are required to stand by or sit on their beds while all detainees are counted—a procedure that can sometimes last an hour or longer. The Commission's survey of facilities holding asylum seekers found that detainees were counted on average five times a day.[77] At the El Paso Service Processing Center, detainees are counted up to nine times a day, according to information provided to Human Rights First staff during a 2006 visit of the facility. At the Elizabeth Detention Center in New Jersey, detainees are counted eight times a day, including three times while detainees are usually asleep.[78] The Commission's expert on criminal prisons—citing to numerous detainee counts as one of the factors—concluded that the detention facilities used "correctional models of security, surveillance, and control."[79] In addition, Human Rights First staff has consistently observed asylum seekers and other detainees being referred to and called by guards by their "bed number" or their "alien registration" number, rather than by their name.

"They gave me a uniform; they told me it was the law. A blue shirt and blue pants and shoes. It's detention but it's as if you're in prison. By being in uniform, we're identified as being the prisoners."

Refugee from Haiti who was granted asylum after four months at the Elizabeth Detention Center in New Jersey

"We need to change our clothes, and then they [immigration officers] give us their uniform. The blue pants and the white T-shirt. We reached the American border and you cross the border, and my understanding was that you would be very safe there. Why was I still being treated in a criminal way? The immigration officer asked me to take a shower. I said, I can't, because I'm very cold. So I changed my clothes and they gave us one blanket, and one pillow case, and one bed sheet, and then they put us in the cell room."

Refugee woman from Burma who requested asylum at the Texas border and was detained at the El Paso Detention Center for more than two years

"The jail guards told us to take off all of our clothes, and then take showers. After showering, I was standing there naked, and then I was given a prison uniform. The whole process was surprising to me, and very embarrassing, but when you're in jail, you have to do as you are told."

Refugee from Somalia who requested asylum at the border and was detained at the Otay Mesa Detention Center in San Diego, California, for four months before being granted asylum

Lack of Privacy. In many of the detention centers and jails, asylum seekers have little or no privacy. Detainees are often housed in large "pods," or dormitories, some holding up to 100 people. At some facilities—like the Willacy, Pearsall, and Northwest detention centers, and the Piedmont county jail in Virginia—detainees sleep in narrow metal triple-bunk beds. (ICE has since stopped detaining asylum seekers and immigrants at the Piedmont jail; following the November 2008 death of an immigrant detainee who was held there, ICE transferred its detainees from the jail.) In some of the facilities, bathroom and toilet areas are separated from the living, sleeping and eating area only by a low wall. Toilet and shower stalls often do not have doors. This is the case at the Willacy and Pearsall detention centers in Texas, the Northwest Detention Center in Washington, and the Elizabeth Detention Center in New Jersey. At the Northwest Detention Center, some of the toilets are reported to be located next to the dining area.[80]

Many of the facilities lack meaningful outdoor space. This is the outdoor recreation area at the Hampton Roads Regional Jail in Virginia.

Lack of Meaningful Outdoor Space. Some of the largest detention facilities do not have meaningful outdoor recreation space for asylum seekers and other immigrant detainees. For example at the Elizabeth Detention Center, the San Diego Detention Center, and the Pearsall Detention Center, asylum seekers and other immigrant detainees only have access to internal courtyards or smaller areas that allow fresh air to enter through a cage-like ceiling, yet are enclosed by the facility's high walls. At a meeting held at the Elizabeth detention facility in July 2007, a local minister raised a concern about the lack of real outdoor space at the facility. The facility's superintendent indicated that the possibility of creating an outdoor recreation area was being considered. Religious leaders who visited the facility again in July 2008 reported that nothing had changed. Now, nearly two years later, the facility still has no meaningful outdoor space.[81] There is more than enough space to construct a true outdoor recreation area at the Pearsall facility, which is surrounded by 35 acres of grass and fields.[82] However detainees there only have access to concrete courtyards off their pods with a mesh ceiling. On the positive side, Human Rights First staff were told by ICE officials, during a visit to the facility, that detainees generally have access to the courtyards throughout the day.

> *"I never had the opportunity to go outside. One hour a day we were allowed to play volleyball in a room where the ceiling is open and covered by iron bars but you can see the sun."*
>
> Refugee from Tibet who was imprisoned by Chinese authorities for more than a year, and then was detained for 11 months at the Elizabeth Detention Center in New Jersey before being granted asylum

At other facilities—like the Varick Street Federal Detention Facility in New York City and the Hampton Roads Regional Jail in Virginia—asylum seekers and other detained immigrants only have access to indoor gyms with high windows as their recreation space.[83] During a visit by Human Rights First staff to the Hampton Roads jail in November 2008, the superintendent acknowledged that the gyms are considered to be outdoor recreation space by ICE, but then added, "I'm not sure how." The Detention Standards only state that "every effort shall be made to place a detainee in a facility that provides outdoor recreation," and define "outdoor recreation" as an open-air space for exercise and other leisure activities.[84] They further provide that someone held at a facility without an outdoor space may request a transfer after six months. Some facilities do have true outdoor recreation areas. For example, the Willacy Detention Center has an outdoor recreation area for each tent, although surrounded by high fences and barbed wire, and the Broward Transitional Center also has open grassy courtyards. The T. Don Hutto Residential Facility—a "family" detention center in Taylor, Texas—also has a true outdoor recreation area surrounded by a barbed wire fence, including tables, a soccer field and two jungle gyms for the children who are detained at the facility.[85]

Family Visits Through Partitions. Many of these facilities do not allow detainees to have contact visits with family or friends. At the Elizabeth Detention Center in New Jersey—a facility that exclusively holds non-criminal detainees—detainees are only allowed to see their family members and friends through a thick sheet of glass, and can only speak to them through a phone. The Pearsall Detention Center, a 1,904-bed facility located in a sparsely populated area one hour from San Antonio, holds hundreds of asylum seekers from all over the world on any given day.[86] Family and friends—who are likely to have traveled a great distance—are only allowed to visit their loved ones through a glass partition. None of the ICE-run and contract detention facilities allow for contact visits with family or friends, with the exception of the Broward Transitional Center.[87] Facilities where contact visits with family and friends are not allowed include the Florence Service Processing Center in Florence, Arizona; the Hampton Roads Regional Jail in Hanover, Virginia; the Krome Service Processing Center in Miami; the Northwest Detention Center in Tacoma, Washington; the Varick Street Federal Detention Facility in New York City; and the Willacy Detention Center in Raymondville, Texas.

Many of the facilities do not allow detainees to have contact visits. Rather, detainees are only allowed to see their family and friends through plexi-glass.

Government Commission: Prison-Like Facilities Inappropriate for Asylum Seekers

In its 2005 study, the bipartisan U.S. Commission on International Religious Freedom found that most of the facilities used by ICE to detain asylum seekers are jails or jail-like facilities that are inappropriate for asylum seekers.[88] The Commission retained an expert on criminal prisons and conducted extensive site visits and a survey of detention facilities. Based on the expert's research, the Commission concluded that the DHS detention standards—that apply to a range of matters including telephone access, visitation, the use of physical restraints, legal orientation presentation access, and outdoor recreation—are "virtually identical to, and indeed are based on, correctional standards."[89]

The Commission's study concluded that "the overwhelming majority of asylum seekers referred for credible fear are detained—for weeks or months and occasionally years—in penal or penitentiary-like facilities."[90] The Commission also found that these detention facilities are "structured and operated much like standardized correctional facilities" and "resemble, in every essential respect, conventional jails."[91]

At these facilities, the Commission found:

- Widespread use of segregation, isolation, or solitary confinement for disciplinary reasons;

- Significant limitations on the privacy, personal freedom, and individuality afforded to detainees;

- A scarcity of private, individual toilets and showers for detainee use outside the presence of others;

- Use of physical restraints on detainees in 18 of the 19 facilities;

- Sight and/or sound surveillance in virtually all housing units, and 24-hour surveillance lighting in all units;

- Security related searches of all detainees in the general living and housing areas; and

- Multiple "counts" throughout the day to monitor detainees' whereabouts at all but one of the facilities visited.

The Commission recommended that asylum seekers be held in "non-jail-like" facilities, and that DHS create detention standards tailored to the needs of asylum seekers and survivors of torture.[92] The Commission cited the Broward Transitional Center in Florida as a model of a less-restrictive—yet secure—form of detention for those asylum seekers who cannot be released. In that facility, asylum seekers can move around and access outdoor areas more freely, and the visitation policy permits contact visits with family and friends. According to the Commission, such a model—while still clearly a form of detention—strikes "a much more appropriate balance between security concerns and the mental health and emotional needs of asylum seekers," and could be replicated in other locations.[93] In its 2007 report on DHS's progress in implementing its recommendations, the Commission pointed out that the Broward facility remained an exception to the penal model used by ICE, and could be used as a model, but that the overwhelming majority of asylum seekers continued to be detained in jail-like facilities.[94] (Though the facility is less jail-like than others, asylum seekers and immigrant detainees held at the Broward facility have faced difficulties in securing medical care and legal representation, as do asylum seekers detained at other facilities.)[95]

> *"While we appreciate the new, performance-based standards of detention developed by the U.S. Immigration and Customs Enforcement (ICE) agency, we do not believe that these standards address our concerns or recommendations. These standards, which are not legally binding, rely on correctional standards, which are inappropriate to asylum seekers."*
>
> U.S. Commission on International Religious Freedom letter to DHS, January 2009

In November 2008, nearly four years after USCIRF issued its February 2005 report, DHS responded to the Commission's concerns and recommendations by citing to ICE's release of the "Performance Based National Detention Standards" in 2008, which will be fully implemented in 2010. These standards, however, like the previous detention standards, continue to be based on the penal model and on standards for correctional institutions. They do not, for example, limit detention to non-jail-like facilities, or require that asylum seekers or other detainees be allowed to wear their own clothes, have real outdoor access, move about within the facility, and visit with family and friends face-to-face rather than through a glass partition.

Facilities opened by ICE

Between FY 2005 and FY 2008, ICE has increased the amount of detention beds by 78%.[96]

Over 6,000 beds were added by ICE in fiscal year 2006 alone. Below are just some of the facilities opened by ICE since it took over immigration enforcement in March 2003.

- South Texas Detention Center (Texas, May 2005): **1,020 beds, expanded to 1,904 beds**

- Willacy Detention Center (Texas, July 2006): **2,000 beds, expanded to 3,000 beds** in June 2008[97]

- Stewart Detention Center (Georgia, October 2006): **1,524 beds**[98]

- T. Don Hutto Family Detention Center (Texas, May 2006): **512 beds**[99]

- Northwest Detention Center (Washington, April 2004): **1,030 beds**[100]

- Bristol Detention Center (Massachusetts, April 2007): **128 beds**[101]

- LaSalle (Jena) Detention Center (Louisiana, November 2007): **1,160 beds**[102]

- Otero County Processing Center (New Mexico, June 2008): **1,088 beds**[103]

Expected Expansions and Pending Proposals

- Farmville detention facility (Virginia, to be operated by contractor Immigration Centers of America, expected to open June 2009): **1,040 beds with potential expansion to 2,500 beds**[104]

- Los Angeles detention facility (California, ICE solicited offers for facility): **2,200 beds**[105]

- Mustang Ridge Family Detention (Texas, proposal by city pending): **200 beds**[106]

- Aurora Contract Detention Facility (Colorado, expansion proposal by contractor GEO pending): **1,100 beds**[107]

- Maverick County Detention Center (Texas, contract between county and GEO, scheduled to open in late 2008): **650 beds**[108]

- Washington State detention facility (Washington, ICE solicited contractor bids in December 2008): **1,575 beds**[109]

- North Georgia Detention Center (Hall County, finalizing intergovernmental service agreement between ICE and contractor CCA): **511 beds**[110]

The New Mega-Jails

Instead of decreasing the use of prison-like facilities, DHS has actually expanded its use of this kind of detention center in the last few years. In 2003, the largest detention centers held at most 300 detainees. Since then, ICE has swiftly opened several mammoth-sized facilities, each holding more than 1,000 detainees and—in the case of the Willacy Detention Center in Raymondville, Texas—up to 3,000 detainees. Between 2005 and 2008 alone, ICE increased detention beds by 78 percent.[111] Furthermore, ICE is seeking funding for an additional 1,000 beds during fiscal year 2010,[112] and there are several reports of new facilities being considered by ICE, including one in rural Virginia and one in Georgia.[113] Human Rights First visited both the Willacy Detention Center as well as the South Texas (Pearsall) Detention Center, and interviewed asylum seekers held at these and two other mega-facilities.

Pearsall Detention Center—Pearsall, Texas

In June 2005, ICE opened the South Texas Detention Center in the town of Pearsall, Texas. The facility was built and is managed by the private contractor GEO Group. Originally designed to house 1,020 detainees, the facility was quickly expanded in 2006 to hold 1,904 immigrants and asylum seekers. The main hallway in the facility—along which all the pods are located—runs about a quarter of a mile long, and detainees are housed in "pods" with as many as 100 beds each.[114]

The facility holds a wide range of immigration detainees, including asylum seekers. ICE staff at the facility and local legal providers told Human Rights First that asylum seekers held at this facility come from a number of countries including Burma, China, Eritrea, Ethiopia, Honduras, Iraq, and Somalia. According to data provided by ICE, more than 2,700 asylum seekers were detained at the facility during the course of fiscal year 2007 alone. ICE did not provide information about how many additional asylum seekers were detained at the facility during that year. This facility is yet another prison-like detention center, complete with prison uniforms, barbed wire, and daily detainee counts. Asylum seekers and other detainees are handcuffed when brought to and from the facility and have little to no privacy in their cell-like "pods." Just as in the other prison-like facilities, the asylum seekers and immigrant detainees are not provided with contact visits and must instead visit with family and friends through glass partitions, speaking through a telephone.

Willacy Detention Center—Raymondville, Texas

In July 2006, ICE opened its largest detention center to date—the Willacy Detention Center—now with 3,000 beds—in Raymondville, Texas. Human Rights First and a delegation of *pro bono* attorneys and representatives of local faith and community groups visited the facility in May 2008 and met with local ICE officials. The Willacy Detention Center primarily consists of ten large tents—white Kevlar fabric stretched over a frame of large steel beams. Each tent is separated into four "pods," each with only one small window. Each pod holds 50 individuals. The detention center is run by the Management Training Corporation (MTC), one of several large private for-profit corrections companies that contract with ICE to provide detention space.

In June 2008, ICE and MTC expanded the original 2,000-bed facility by adding an adjacent building that can hold 1,000 detainees. Both the "tent" and building areas of the facility are essentially jails. The detainees wear jail uniforms, and the facility is surrounded by high barbed wire fences. In both the tents and in the building, detainees are held in "pods" with the eating, sleeping, and toilet area all in one room. The toilet and shower areas are separated from the eating, sleeping and living areas only by a low wall. Immigration detainees are not permitted contact visits and instead communicate with visitors through a glass partition. There are only three attorney visitation rooms, all of which are non-contact rooms that resemble tiny closets or confessionals. This not only makes it difficult for attorneys to build a relationship of trust with their clients, but it also means that every time a document needs to be handed between the detainee and the attorney, the document must first be given to the guard who then walks it around to the other party. Attorneys are sometimes allowed to use empty courtrooms to meet with their clients.[115]

During its May 2008 visit to the Willacy facility, Human Rights First was told by ICE officers that the facility is primarily used to hold immigrant detainees who are subject to expedited removal. Many asylum seekers who are placed in expedited removal in the southwest Texas border area are initially detained at Willacy before being transferred to another facility, often the Pearsall Detention Center, for their credible fear interviews.

According to data provided to Human Rights First by ICE, approximately 550 asylum seekers were detained at Willacy over the course of 2007. In April and May 2008 alone, over 140 asylum seekers subject to expedited removal were initially detained at Willacy.[116] Asylum seekers from many countries have been held at the facility, including some from Burma, China, El Salvador, Haiti, Nicaragua, and Somalia. ICE officials informed Human Rights First during the tour of the facility that the majority of the detainees are in the process of being deported by ICE, with many being in expedited removal, and that the average stay for those in expedited removal was only 18 days. ICE officials also provided data indicating that the average length of detention for asylum seekers at Willacy was only seven days. Asylum seekers are often transferred to other facilities for their credible fear interviews and any subsequent asylum hearings. During its visit of the facility, Human Rights First met with one asylum seeker who had spent over four months at the Willacy Detention Center.

Stewart Detention Center—Lumpkin, Georgia

Yet another massive detention center opened its doors in the fall of 2006. The Stewart Detention Center is a 1,524-bed medium security facility, constructed and managed by the Corrections Corporation of America (CCA)—one of the largest private correctional corporations—"in response to demand for prison and detainee beds."[117] The facility holds only men. It is located in rural Lumpkin, Georgia, and often holds detainees who have been transferred there from other parts of the country, especially from the nearby states of North Carolina, South Carolina, and Tennessee, but sometimes also from states farther away.[118] For example, a number of immigration detainees reported to Human Rights First that they had been transferred to this facility for several weeks or months before being returned to detention in New Jersey, generally for deportation.[119] ICE officers have cited bed space needs for these transfers, but it may be that detainees are transferred to other locations because detention space outside of the East Coast is less expensive.

The detention center is located three hours from Atlanta. There are few legal service providers in the area, and even fewer that work at the detention center. Because the roundtrip six-hour drive cannot easily be done in one day, the Catholic Charities of Atlanta attorney who conducts the legal orientation presentations at the facility, must spend two nights each week in a hotel close to the facility.[120]

Northwest Detention Center—Tacoma, Washington

The Northwest Detention Center (NWDC) in Tacoma, Washington, was opened in April 2004, and is operated by the private corporation GEO Group. ICE's original contract was for 500 beds, but the facility now has the capacity to hold 1,000 individuals, both men and women. According to a report issued in July 2008 by OneAmerica and the Seattle University School of Law International Human Rights Clinic, a significant number of detainees are held for 35-60 days at the facility. One asylum seeker identified in the report had been detained for more than four years before being granted asylum by the U.S. immigration court.[121]

Like other large immigration detention facilities, detainees at NWDC are given prison uniforms and are held in pods that lack any meaningful privacy, with toilets and showers only separated from the sleeping quarters by low dividers. Contact visits with family members or friends are not allowed—instead, detainees can only speak with their visitors through a heavy glass partition and a phone.[122]

The detention center is located approximately 45 minutes from Seattle, where a few immigration legal service providers are located. The facility was designed with only four attorney-client meeting rooms, and no modifications were made when the number of beds was doubled to 1,000. As a result, the OneAmerica and Seattle University School of Law study reports that *pro bono* attorneys experience long wait times when they visit their clients.[123]

Continued Detention in Jails

"I was crying in jail. I was hungry. I was surprised to be in jail. I had never committed a crime, and suddenly I was in jail."

> Refugee from Ethiopia who was detained for six months at the Piedmont jail in Virginia before being granted asylum by a U.S. immigration court

In addition to detaining asylum seekers and immigrants in large immigration detention centers, ICE also contracts bed-space from more than 500 local jails.[124] In fact, in recent years, ICE has increased its use of local jails. Between 2002 and 2006, the number of immigration detainees held in local jails or Federal Bureau of Prisons facilities increased by 30.7 percent.[125] Between 2006 and 2007 alone—as the overall number of immigration

detainees grew—the number of detainees held at local jails jumped from 45 percent to 65 percent.[126] Because these facilities also house criminal inmates, they function fully as jails. In some cases, immigration detainees are housed together with the criminal population. This was the case at both the Hampton Roads Regional Jail and the Piedmont County Jail in Virginia when Human Rights First staff visited both jails in November 2008. Asylum seekers and other immigration detainees held at these facilities were largely subject to the same schedule and conditions as the criminal inmates: they wore jail uniforms, were subject to regular counts, and had only limited outdoor recreation time.

Some of these jails, including Hampton Roads and Piedmont, are in remote or rural areas. These two facilities, for example, are located three or more hours from the *pro bono* legal representation organization—the Washington, DC based CAIR Coalition—that provides legal orientation presentations and free representation to asylum seekers. ICE deportation officers are not stationed at either of these jails, like they usually are at contract facilities that hold only immigration detainees.[127] Detainees at both of the jails Human Rights First visited in Virginia—which included asylum seekers from Burundi, China, Ethiopia, and Zimbabwe—reported that they relied on weekly visits by ICE officers to communicate with the officers and to obtain information on the status of their cases. Some detainees expressed frustration at not having more regular contact with ICE. According to local *pro bono* attorneys, detainees express similar concerns at several jails in Illinois and Minnesota.

More Family Detention Facilities

In 2001, the former INS began detaining immigrant families in the Berks County Shelter Care Facility in Pennsylvania, a former nursing home with space for 84 men, women, and children. Concerned about the separation of families, the House Committee on Appropriations stated in a 2005 report that DHS was expected to "release families or use alternatives to detention...whenever possible," and directed that when the detention of family units was determined to be necessary, the family members should be housed together, to avoid the separation of parents from young children.[128]

In May 2006, ICE opened the T. Don Hutto Residential Facility in Taylor, Texas, a former prison designated specifically to detain immigrants, asylum seekers, and their children.[129] This 512-bed facility located outside Austin, Texas, was originally built as a medium-security prison, and is operated by the private contractor Corrections Corporation of America (CCA). The facility has housed asylum seekers from Guatemala, Haiti, Honduras, Iraq, Nicaragua, Romania, Somalia, and Venezuela—and their families.[130] When the facility first opened, asylum seekers and other immigrant families were held in cells, each with a single bed or a bunk bed. Family groups were not always housed in the same cell. All detainees—including the children—wore prison-like uniforms. School-age children received only one hour of education per day, and outdoor recreation was limited.[131] In a February 2007 report, the Lutheran Immigration and Refugee Service (LIRS) and the Women's Refugee Commission documented these and other problems at the facility. Local community and faith-based groups also voiced concern with immigration authorities and the media about the treatment of families detained at the Hutto facility.[132]

Following initial criticism of the facility, ICE made several adjustments, including expanding the instruction period for children from one to four hours a day.[133] In March 2007, the American Civil Liberties Union (ACLU), the University of Texas School of Law Immigration Clinic, and the law firm of LeBoeuf, Lamb, Greene & MacRae LLP filed a lawsuit, alleging that conditions at the facility violated the minimum standards for the detention of minors in immigration custody. In an August 2007 settlement of that lawsuit, DHS agreed to implement a number of changes,

including no longer requiring children or their parents to wear prison uniforms, replacing guard uniforms with khakis and polo shirts, improving privacy and living arrangements, allowing freedom of movement inside the facility, and more time for outdoor recreation and education.[134] The settlement agreement, however, is set to expire in August 2009.

The Hutto settlement also requires that ICE make reasonable efforts to reduce the length of detention and provide written individualized custody determinations after 60 days and every 30 days thereafter. In fact, local legal providers report that average length of detention for families detained at Hutto was initially shortened significantly following the settlement, but has already begun to increase, with families who are seeking asylum remaining in detention for two to six months.[135]

ICE continues to detain asylum seekers and their children at the Hutto facility. ICE also continues to detain families at the smaller Berks County Shelter Care Facility. At this facility, families have access to true outdoor recreation and the education provided to children was reported to be appropriate. At the same time, though, the Women's Refugee Commission and LIRS found that children as young as six were sometimes separated in different sleeping areas from their parents.[136] The UNHCR Guidelines on Protection and Care of Refugee Children state that "refugee children should not be detained," and that children should not be detained in prison-like conditions, and that "because detention can be very harmful to refugee children, it must be 'used only as a measure of last resort and for the shortest appropriate period of time.'"[137]

*In April 2007, **a family of Iraqi Christians**—parents and a two year old baby girl—arrived at the Mexico-California border, approached a U.S. immigration officer and requested asylum. They were immediately detained and sent to the Hutto detention center in Texas. The mother and the* daughter were separated from the father and placed in a different dormitory. For much of their detention, the family was not allowed free movement within the facility. They, like all the other detainees, had to stay in their small pod for most of the day, and were forced to line up and be counted several times each day. The family was represented pro bono by an attorney from Catholic Charities of Austin, who requested on several occasions that the family be released on parole. The Catholic Charities attorney even called the ICE Field Office Director to follow up on her requests, but never received a response. The family was detained for over five months. They were only released from detention following the August 2007 settlement.[138] The family was granted asylum by a U.S. immigration judge in August 2008.

In January 2008, ICE issued a new set of standards governing the detention of immigrant families. While the new standards improve access to phones and increase access to the law library,[139] the new standards continue to be based on adult correctional standards. In a June 2008 statement, the Women's Refugee Commission pointed out, for example, that these standards "allow children to be disciplined based on adult prison protocol, including the use of restraints...and strip searches."[140]

In April 2008, ICE solicited bids for contracts to construct three additional 200-bed facilities to detain immigrant families.[141] Though the ICE solicitation described the facilities as "minimal security for juveniles and their families,"[142] ICE's request also called for the use of penal-type security mechanisms such as fencing and physical counts.[143]

Penal Detention Inappropriate Under International Standards

"While the agency's detention standards do not exactly mirror the proposed standards of the United Nations or the International standards reflected in the [USCIRF] report, we are confident that they do meet our obligation to ensure proper treatment and conditions of confinement."

ICE response to the U.S. Commission on International Religious Freedom's report, January 2009

The United States, as a signatory to the 1967 Protocol Relating to the Status of Refugees, is bound by Articles 2 through 34 of the 1951 Convention Relating to the Status of Refugees.[144] Article 31 of the 1951 Refugee Convention exempts refugees from being punished because of their illegal entry or presence. It also provides that states shall not unnecessarily restrict the movements of entering asylum seekers.

The Executive Committee of the United Nations High Commissioner for Refugees (UNHCR), of which the United States is a member, has concluded that detention of asylum seekers "should normally be avoided." The Executive Committee has also urged that national legislation and/or administrative practice distinguish between the situation of asylum seekers and that of other aliens, and that asylum seekers not be housed with criminal inmates.[145]

In February 1999, the UNHCR issued revised Guidelines on the Detention of Asylum Seekers (the "UNHCR Guidelines"). The UNHCR Guidelines affirm that "[a]s a general rule, asylum seekers should not be detained," and that "the use of detention is, in many instances, contrary to the norms and principles of international law." The UNHCR Guidelines also specifically emphasize that "[t]he use of prisons should avoided." When asylum seekers are detained, the UNHCR Guidelines recommend "the use of separate detention facilities to accommodate asylum-seekers." The guidelines also caution: "Detention of asylum seekers which is applied as part of a policy to deter future asylum seekers, or to dissuade those who have commenced their claims from pursuing them, is contrary to the norms of refugee law. It should not be used as a punitive or disciplinary measure for illegal entry or presence in the country."[146]

Failure to Adopt Safeguards to Ensure Fairness

"I was so sad, I did not know what is going to happen with my family in Afghanistan, with me here in the United States and I did not know anything about asylum. The only thing was in my mind to save my life and my family's. I thought...[the United States] might welcome me, protect me and give me freedom, but I was wrong."

Refugee from Afghanistan who fled from the Taliban and was detained for 20 months at three different county jails in Illinois and Wisconsin. He was denied parole on two occasions and only released after he was found eligible for asylum.

Those who seek asylum at our airports and borders are placed into "mandatory detention" under the "expedited removal" process. They are only permitted to apply for asylum if they first pass a "credible fear" screening interview with a U.S. asylum officer, or a subsequent review by an immigration judge. Those who "pass" this interview are technically eligible to request release from detention on "parole."[147] Unlike other immigrant detainees, however, these asylum seekers—who are labeled as "arriving aliens" under our immigration system—are not given the opportunity to have an immigration court custody hearing to assess their eligibility for release.[148] Rather, the decision as to their release on parole or their continued detention rests with ICE—the same authority that is responsible for their detention.

Since DHS and ICE took over responsibility for immigration detention in 2003, the flawed asylum detention system has become more restrictive, leaving asylum seekers sitting in jails for months or even longer. As detailed below:

- The rate of release on parole for asylum seekers dropped from 41.3 percent to 4.2 percent between 2004 and 2007.

- ICE issued a more restrictive parole policy for asylum seekers in November 2007—a policy that is inconsistent with the recommendations of the bipartisan U.S. Commission on International Religious Freedom.

- In interviews with Human Rights First researchers, *pro bono* attorneys who work with refugees across the country reported that in almost all locations their clients experienced no improvements under the new ICE policy.

- In Massachusetts, Texas, and Arizona, some detained asylum seekers have not been given their credible fear interviews for several weeks or even months, delaying their ability to apply for release on parole.

- The U.S. detention system for asylum seekers is out of step with international refugee protection and human rights standards.

As a result of U.S. detention policies and practices, refugees who seek asylum in this country are jailed for extended periods of time—even when they meet the criteria for release on parole. For example, Human Rights First attorneys have interviewed:

■ A Baptist Chin woman from Burma who was detained in an El Paso, Texas, immigration jail for more than two years. Several parole requests were denied by ICE even though she had proof of her identity and family in the U.S. and the U.S. government agreed that she would be subjected to torture if returned to Burma. She was finally released on parole from detention and was subsequently granted asylum.

■ A human rights advocate who was detained for four months at the Elizabeth Detention Center in New Jersey. The advocate fled Guinea after being abducted by government forces on two occasions due to his involvement with and founding of several human rights organizations. He was finally released on parole but only three weeks before a U.S. immigration judge granted him asylum.

■ A Liberian Pentecostal pastor who was detained in the U.S. for three and a half months and denied parole, even though several ministers in the U.S. confirmed his identity and his religious work in Liberia. In Liberia, he had been targeted by the regime of Charles Taylor because he had criticized the use of child soldiers. He was only released from detention after he was granted asylum.

A Flawed Process

The U.S. immigration detention system lacks the safeguards necessary to ensure that detention is consistent with this country's moral commitment to protect the victims of persecution and its legal commitments under international refugee and human rights conventions. For example:

■ The initial determination to detain an asylum seeker at a U.S. airport or border point is a blanket "mandatory" one, not based on an individualized determination, but rather on whether a person possesses valid documents.[149]

■ Subsequent decisions to release asylum seekers on parole are entrusted to ICE, which is the detaining authority, rather than to an independent authority or court.[150]

■ The parole criteria that are specific to asylum seekers are set forth in an ICE policy directive rather than the relevant regulations, and allow the continued detention of an asylum seeker even where she or he has established identity, community ties, and lack of flight risk or danger to the community.[151]

■ The system fails to provide for regular review of the need for continued detention although asylum seekers' cases may take months or even years to make their way through the adjudication system.[152]

ICE acts, in effect, as both judge and jailer with respect to parole decisions for asylum seekers. If parole is denied by ICE, the decision cannot be appealed to a judge—even an immigration judge. While immigration judges can review ICE custody decisions for other immigration detainees, they are precluded under regulatory language from reviewing the detention of so-called "arriving aliens," a group that includes asylum seekers who arrive at airports and other U.S. entry points.[153] While asylum seekers have

Arbitrary Detention Under International Law

The U.S. detention system for asylum seekers lacks the kinds of safeguards that prevent detention from being arbitrary within the meaning of the International Covenant on Civil and Political Rights (ICCPR). The ICCPR, to which the United States is a party, provides that "Anyone who is deprived of his liberty by arrest or detention shall be entitled to take proceedings before a court, in order that the court may decide without delay on the lawfulness of his detention and order his release if the detention is not lawful."[154] The U.N. Human Rights Committee, in examining the detention of a Cambodian asylum seeker in Australia, concluded that detention should be considered arbitrary "if it is not necessary in all the circumstances of the case."[155]

The UNHCR Executive Committee, of which the United States is a member, has "[r]ecommended that detention measures taken in respect of refugees and asylum-seekers should be subject to judicial or administrative review."[156] The UNHCR guidelines on the detention of asylum seekers state that "as a general principle, asylum-seekers should not be detained." When a decision to detain is made, the UNHCR guidelines call for procedural safeguards including "automatic review before a judicial or administrative body independent of the detaining authorities." In addition to this automatic independent review, the decision should be subject to subsequent "regular periodic reviews of the necessity for the continuance of detention."[157]

After a 2007 mission to the United States, the U.N. Special Rapporteur on the Human Rights of Migrants concluded that the U.S. detention system lacks safeguards that prevent detention from being arbitrary within the meaning of the ICCPR and, among other things, recommended that DHS and DOJ "revise regulations to make clear that asylum-seekers can request [their] custody determinations from immigration judges."[158]

occasionally tried to file federal court habeas petitions to challenge parole denials, these petitions do not serve as an effective mechanism for asylum seekers to obtain a timely and independent review of ICE decisions to deny them parole. Practically speaking, it can take months or longer before a decision is issued in these cases.[159] Some

federal courts have refused to review parole denials for asylum seekers, in some cases citing a lack of jurisdiction and in other cases emphasizing that they are obligated to defer to the judgment of immigration officials as long as a reason was given for the parole denial.[160]

Failure to Implement Critical Reforms

In its 2005 report, the U.S. Commission on International Religious Freedom found wide variations in asylum parole rates across the country based on its analysis of DHS statistics. This statistical analysis showed that while asylum seekers in some parts of the country were routinely released, in other parts of the country, asylum seekers were rarely paroled—with parole rates as low as 0.5 percent in New Orleans, 3.8 percent in New Jersey, and 8 percent in New York.[161] The Commission also found no evidence that ICE was applying the parole criteria that were spelled out in the policy guidelines in effect at the time: which included establishing identity, community ties and no security risk. Rather, the Commission concluded that variations in parole rates were associated with other factors, including, for instance, the airport or border entry post at which the asylum seeker had arrived.[162]

The Commission specifically recommended that DHS promulgate regulations "to promote more consistent implementation of existing parole criteria, [and] to ensure that asylum seekers with credible fear of persecution...are released from detention." The Commission also recommended that ICE create "standardized forms and national review procedures" to ensure that the parole criteria are applied uniformly.[163]

ICE did not, however, put the parole criteria into regulations. In a February 2007 "report card," USCIRF gave ICE a grade of "F" for its failure to codify the parole criteria into regulations and another "F" for its failure to ensure consistent and correct parole decisions by developing standardized forms and national review procedures.[164]

ICE's New Asylum Parole Policy

Instead of putting the prior asylum parole criteria into regulations, ICE rescinded those guidelines in November 2007 and issued new guidance that inserted an additional level of eligibility requirements for release on parole.[165] The new directive makes it clear that meeting the previous parole criteria—establishing identity, community ties, and no security risk—is no longer enough. An asylum seeker must also establish that:

- there are medical reasons which warrant release,

- s/he is a juvenile or a government witness in a legal proceeding, or that

- the release would be "in the public interest."

The prior parole guidance was based on the premise that parole of an asylum seeker who can establish identity and community ties, and who is not a threat to the safety of the community, is generally in the public interest and should be favored.[166] The new guidance states that asylum seekers are only to be paroled in "limited circumstances."[167] In a December 3, 2007, letter to Human Rights First concerning the new parole policy, former ICE Assistant Secretary Julie L. Myers stated that the "blanket statements," which she said were contained in the earlier parole policy, "placed an undue burden on our agency when denying parole for justifiable reasons, creating an inflexible adjudicatory process that was inappropriate to continue after the September 11, 2001, terrorist attacks."[168] The prior guidance, however, had clearly authorized release only when the asylum seeker did not pose a security risk.[169]

Not only did ICE shift its overall policy approach towards parole of asylum seekers, but it also restricted the number of asylum seekers to whom it applies. Unlike the prior guidelines, ICE's new parole guidance does not require that all asylum seekers be assessed for release to ensure that those who can and should be released are not unnecessarily detained. Instead, asylum seekers must submit a written request for parole before being considered for release.[170] This approach disadvantages individuals who do not speak English or are not represented—and more than a third of asylum seekers in detention are not represented.[171] These individuals are less likely to learn about the parole process or to be able to make a formal written application.

The new directive did create an additional requirement that local offices gather and submit monthly reports on parole determinations, and that a "thorough and objective quality assurance review" should be undertaken every six months. Nevertheless, this new policy guidance—like the parole policy guidance that preceded it—has not been placed into regulations. As a result, it leaves local officials with the ability to disregard it, as they did the prior guidance.[172] Moreover, while the "public interest" category could be—and has in some cases been—used in an officer's discretion to release asylum seekers who do not fall into any of the other narrow categories, the guidance fails to provide any meaningful explanation as to who would qualify for parole under the "public interest" criteria—leaving the decision up to the discretion of local officers.

Though ICE framed the new guidance as a response to USCIRF's recommendations, in a letter dated December 14, 2007, the Chair of the Commission wrote to former ICE Assistant Secretary Julie Myers stating that the new policy is "inconsistent with the relevant recommendation of the Commission's Study."[173] The Commission specifically requested that ICE stop citing the Commission's recommendations as the basis for the new policy. The Commission reiterated these concerns in a January 2009 letter to Stewart Baker, then DHS Assistant Secretary for Policy.[174] In a February 2008 letter, 82 nonprofit organiza-

ticers and legal experts expressed concern about the new directive and called for ICE to rescind it.[175]

Reform More Necessary Than Ever

"[A]liens are only to be paroled in limited circumstances."

ICE Directive on Parole of Asylum Seekers
(November 2007)

In the years since DHS took over responsibility for the detention of asylum seekers, the overall release rate and the rate of release on parole for asylum seekers appear to have dipped sharply. ICE statistics obtained by USCIRF indicated that the rate of release for asylum seekers who are found to have a credible fear of persecution dropped from 86.1 to 62.5 percent between fiscal years 2001 and 2003.[176] Statistics provided to Human Rights First by ICE indicate that the rate of release has further dropped to 44.7 percent in fiscal year 2007. The rate of release on parole has also dropped significantly from 41.3 to 4.2 percent between fiscal years 2004 and 2007.[177]

Other recent—though incomplete—statistics provided by ICE for fiscal year 2008 similarly point to a very low parole rate for asylum seekers. A set of numbers provided by ICE to the U.S. Commission on International Religious Freedom in November 2008 reflect that ICE paroled only 107 asylum seekers, out of the 215 written parole requests submitted, in the eight month period from November 2007 through June 2008—a period in which ICE newly detained 842 arriving asylum seekers who were found to have a credible fear of persecution, over and above the number it continued to hold in detention from the prior years.[178] These limited statistics point to a parole rate that would be somewhere below 13 percent. In an April 2008 letter to Human Rights First, ICE provided a preliminary set of parole statistics to nongovernmental

groups that also pointed to a low parole rate—with only 45 asylum seekers being granted parole in the period from November 2007 through January 2008. In presenting these statistics, ICE did not provide complete information, instead providing the parole rate only as it relates to the number of applications filed, rather than to the number of asylum seekers actually in immigration detention.[179]

ICE's interpretation of parole eligibility—both before and after the new parole guidance was issued—has continued to be restrictive and uneven in practice according to information obtained by Human Rights First through interviews with local legal providers who assist asylum seekers at the facilities that detain the bulk of asylum seekers. *Pro bono* attorneys reported that asylum seekers continued to be detained in facilities in California, Florida, Georgia, Illinois, Louisiana, Minnesota, Oregon, Texas, and other states, even when they could be released on parole—and that asylum seekers they represent are regularly denied parole from detention.

■ **Florida**: The Florida Immigrant Advocacy Center (FIAC), which provides free legal services to detainees at the Krome Detention Center and the Broward Transitional Facility, reported that parole is almost never granted—both before and after the new parole directive was issued—and that they have represented detained asylum seekers whose parole requests went unanswered or denied with little or no explanation.[180]

■ **Illinois, Indiana, and Wisconsin**: A representative from the National Immigrant Justice Center reports that, in her experience, "parole is rarely granted" to asylum seekers who arrive at Chicago's airport and who are then detained in county jails throughout Illinois, Indiana, and Wisconsin, though in her experience individuals from China have more success with parole.[181]

■ **Austin, Texas**: The Immigration Clinic at the University of Texas School of Law, which represents asylum seekers at the Hutto Detention Center, reported that—

while asylum seekers were being regularly paroled following the settlement of the lawsuit surrounding the Hutto Detention Center—many asylum seekers being granted parole are now made to post a $5,000 bond. Some families cannot afford such a high bond, and as a consequence continue to be detained for the duration of their cases. Furthermore, on average it takes three to four weeks to receive a decision on a parole request, meaning that asylum seekers who have already spent several weeks in detention awaiting a credible fear interview and decision, spend almost an additional month in detention awaiting a response to their parole request.[182]

■ **Harlingen, Texas**: A private attorney who represents numerous asylum seekers at the Willacy and Port Isabel Detention Centers in Texas—often on a *pro bono* basis—reported that she knows of nobody who was granted paroled.[183]

■ **Pearsall, Texas**: American Gateways, which provides free representation for asylum seekers detained at the Pearsall Detention Center reported that in 2008 they had not had a single parole request granted for asylum seekers at that facility. They also reported that asylum seekers who are paroled from other facilities—such as the Hutto Detention Center—are sometimes required to post a bond as high as $5,000.[184]

■ **Virginia**: The CAIR Coalition, which represents asylum seekers and others detained in county jails in Virginia, reported that it usually did not receive a response to any formal parole requests submitted on behalf of its clients, and that when asylum seekers were released—sometimes months after the parole request was filed—the attorneys did not always receive notice.[185]

One *pro bono* practitioner from Arizona reported that a local ICE officer, after the issuance of the November 2007 parole guidance, told *pro bono* attorneys that "Parole is available for Mother Teresa."[186]

Through its interviews with legal providers, Human Rights First gathered a number of examples of refugees who were denied or not granted parole in the wake of the new guidance:

■ **An Ethiopian refugee**, who had suffered torture and persecution in his home country because of his Somali ethnic background, was detained at the South Texas Detention Center after he arrived at the U.S. border in early January 2008 and requested asylum. His pro bono attorney requested that he be released from detention on parole, submitting proof of his identity, an affidavit of support from the refugee's U.S. citizen cousin, and proof that he would have a place to live if released. But ICE denied his parole request. The ICE parole denial stated that he "failed to demonstrate [his] parole would be justified for urgent humanitarian reasons or would yield a significant public benefit" and that he did not fall into one of the five categories of asylum seekers eligible for parole—which includes parole in the public interest. The man was detained nearly ten months before being granted asylum by the immigration court. Only then was he finally released from detention.[187]

■ **A Tibetan monk**, who came to the U.S. after suffering persecution due to his involvement in pro-Tibet demonstrations, was detained in Buffalo, New York and then transferred to the Port Isabel Detention Center in south Texas. His attorney filed a request that he be released from detention on parole. The request included proof of his identity and information on a sponsor who was willing to house him. The parole request was denied by ICE with a brief letter stating generically that there was no humanitarian interest in releasing him. The monk remained in detention until he was found eligible for asylum by the Board of Immigration Appeals. He was released after spending a year and a few days in detention.[188]

■ **An asylum seeker from Burma** came to the U.S. border, requesting protection. She was detained and brought to the Pearsall detention center in Texas. She began to experience intestinal bleeding but was only treated with ibuprofen and a topical cream. Her pro bono attorney requested that she be released on parole, providing a letter of support from the woman's cousin who had already been granted asylum in the United States. The pro bono attorney also provided information on his client's medical problems. The request was denied by ICE two weeks later. This Burmese refugee was only released after seven months in detention in this Texas jail—when a U.S. immigration judge granted her request for asylum.[189]

Delays in Credible Fear Interviews Leading to Delays in Parole

Asylum seekers who are detained "mandatorily" under expedited removal can apply for release on parole only *after* they have had a "credible fear" screening interview with a U.S. asylum officer and are subsequently advised that they have met that "credible fear" standard. On average, these credible fear interviews occur within 13 or 14 days of when an asylum seeker's case is referred to the local asylum office, according to statics provided by U.S. Citizenship and Immigration Services, the arm of the Department of Homeland Security that houses the Asylum Division. The referral to the asylum office may take place soon after the asylum seeker is initially detained, but sometimes asylum seekers wait weeks before immigration enforcement authorities refer them for a screening interview.

An average wait time of about two weeks—from the date of referral—obviously implies that some asylum seekers wait longer for these interviews. In conducting research for this report, Human Rights First was informed by *pro bono* attorneys who assist asylum seekers at six different detention facilities and jails in Arizona, Massachusetts,

and Texas that they were aware of asylum seekers who were not given these critical screening interviews for two to six months after their detention. For example, *pro bono* attorneys in Massachusetts reported that they have observed a six-month delay in credible fear interviews. *Pro bono* attorneys in Texas and Arizona, reported that detained asylum seekers sometimes wait a couple of months, and sometimes longer, before receiving a credible fear interview. In February 2009, the Los Angeles asylum office (which has jurisdiction over Arizona, southern California, and Hawaii) advised that detained asylum seekers can expect to wait at least six months before being scheduled for a credible fear interview, according to *pro bono* attorneys who assist asylum seekers in Arizona. Attorneys in Texas report that asylum seekers detained at the Pearsall facility—which detained more than 2,000 credible fear asylum seekers in 2007—often wait two to four months before receiving a screening interview. *Pro bono* attorneys working at the Port Isabel, Willacy, and Hutto detention centers—all in Texas—also reported long delays.[190] These four major Texas detention facilities are all under the jurisdiction of the Houston asylum office.

These excessive waiting times for credible fear interviews delay the ability of an asylum seeker to apply for parole— and also extend the period of the asylum seeker's detention by several weeks or even months.

Prohibitively High Bonds

Bond is often required as a condition of release for asylum seekers and other immigrant detainees. While asylum seekers who are detained at U.S. airports and borders are prevented from having immigration court custody hearings under the current regulations, other asylum seekers and immigrant detainees—those who are detained within the United States—can have the immigration courts review the amount of their bonds in custody hearings. In these custody hearings, they have an opportunity to present evidence—such as that they are not a security threat and that they have community ties—in support of their release.[191] The bond amount is initially set by ICE, and the immigration judge can review this amount and order that the asylum seeker be released on a different bond amount or on his own recognizance.[192] In some jurisdictions, asylum seekers who are eligible for release only on parole have been required to pay bond as an additional condition to their release.

In the course of Human Rights First's interviews with local legal providers, attorneys in Florida, New Mexico, and Texas, reported that they had asylum clients for whom bonds had been set so high—by ICE as well as by the immigration courts—that their clients could not pay them. Through our research we learned of a number of cases of asylum seekers who were not released because they could not pay bonds set at around $5,000, but who were subsequently granted asylum. As a result, even those who are eligible for release on bond may continue to be detained. According to statistics provided by ICE, the average bond set by ICE and immigration judges is almost $6,000, but the figure is significantly higher in some areas, with bonds averaging about $9,000 in the New York and New Jersey areas.[193]

Refugees often face great difficulty in paying bonds, as many have lost their homes and livelihoods in their flight from persecution. Their families too may be stranded in exile abroad, without income or sometimes living in refugee camps.

While fewer asylum seekers are being released, a greater percentage of those who are released are being required to pay a bond as a condition of release. In fact, ICE statistics indidate that while less than 30 percent of asylum seekers released from detention in 2004 were required to post bond, nearly three-quarters of asylum seekers released in 2007 were released on bond, rather than on parole or on their own recognizance.[194]

An Ethiopian refugee was detained at the Pearsall Detention Center in Texas after he crossed the Mexican border in order to seek asylum in the United States. In Ethiopia, he had been tortured and detained after he was falsely accused of taking part in an anti-government protest. Catholic Charities of Austin took on his asylum case on a pro bono basis. The refugee had proof of his identity, no criminal history, and his pro bono attorneys had secured space for him at a local home for refugees. Though he was eligible for release on bond, the bond amount set by ICE was $7,000—too high for him to be able to post. Even after the immigration judge reduced the bond amount significantly to $4,000 in a custody hearing, he still could not afford to pay it. As a result, he was forced to remain in detention for over five months, and was released from detention only after he was granted asylum.[195]

Lengthy Detention

Asylum seekers are often detained for many months, and sometimes for a year or more, while their asylum claims make their way through the adjudication system. Neither U.S. laws nor regulations set a limit on the length of time an asylum seeker may be detained while his or her asylum proceedings are pending.[196]

ICE is required to provide statistics to Congress regarding the "average length of detention and the number of detainees by category of the length of detention."[197] The statistics that ICE has produced, however, do not provide complete information about the length of time that asylum seekers are detained. In particular, due to the manner in which they are generated, these statistics do not reflect longer term detentions. Based on these statistics, USCIRF calculated that approximately a third of arriving asylum seekers were jailed for 90 days or more.[198]

ICE statistics provided to Human Rights First for fiscal year 2006 indicate that at least 1,559 asylum seekers were detained for over six months before being released.[199] This statistic does not, however, include asylum seekers who were still detained at the time the statistics were compiled, nor the additional number of asylum seekers who continued to be detained from prior years. ICE statistics provided to Human Rights First for fiscal year 2007 show that the average length of detention for asylum seekers is 93.8 days, and that at least 2,200 asylum seekers who were taken into custody in 2007 were detained for six months or more. Again though, this number does not include those who were still detained at the time the statistics were compiled, and it does not include information on asylum seekers who were initially detained in a previous fiscal year and continued to be detained in 2007.[200] ICE has not yet provided these statistics for the 2008 fiscal year.

A number of studies have documented examples of lengthy detentions. One study, conducted in 2003, documented an average length of detention of ten months for the 40 asylum seekers whose cases were tracked and were granted asylum by the end of the study.[201] An Associated Press investigation revealed that 400 immigration detainees who did not have criminal convictions had been detained for at least a year as of January 2009—and a dozen had been held for three years or more.[202] Human rights organizations and news reports have documented cases of asylum seekers who have been detained for three, four, and even five years.[203]

During the course of its research, Human Rights First learned of many lengthy detentions. At the Pearsall facility alone, Human Rights First was told by ICE, following its delegation's visit to the facility, that there were 14 asylum seekers who had been detained for more than a year, and an additional 23 who had been detained for six months or

longer.[204] The average length of detention for Human Rights First's latest 40 *pro bono* refugee clients is about five to six months. The refugees interviewed by Human Rights First in the course of our research for this report were detained for an average of nine months before being released. We have also met with several asylum seekers who have been detained for well over a year—including the Burmese Baptist Chin woman who was detained for more than two years who is profiled earlier in this chapter. In addition:

■ A fisherman who was persecuted by the LTTE in Sri Lanka was detained for 30 months in a New Jersey immigration jail before being released from detention and given an electronic monitoring device;[205]

■ An Afghan refugee who fled Taliban threats was detained for a year and a half in three county jails in Illinois and Wisconsin.

Detention After Asylum Seekers Ruled Eligible for Protection

In some instances, asylum seekers have been detained even after an immigration court rules that they have a fear of persecution in their home country and are entitled to relief. *Pro bono* attorneys in Arizona and Florida have reported to Human Rights First that, when ICE attorneys have appealed an immigration judge's decision to grant asylum to the Board of Immigration Appeals, in some instances ICE has continued to detain the asylum seeker while the appeal is pending—a process which often takes several months.[206] For example:

A Colombian refugee, who had been jailed, beaten, and tortured for participating in a political demonstration in Colombia, was detained in a U.S. immigration jail in Arizona for 14 months, including for over eight months after an Immigration

*Judge had ruled that he was eligible for asylum.
The ICE attorney who had argued against the
refugee's asylum request appealed the judge's
decision to the Board of Immigration Appeals. ICE
refused to release the asylum seeker while the
appeal was pending. ICE denied his request for
parole, even though the man had both a U.S.
citizen daughter and a U.S. citizen father. He was
finally released after eight additional months in
detention, over two weeks after the Board of Immigration Appeals affirmed the judge's decision
granting him asylum.*[207]

Previously, it was ICE policy to "favor release of aliens who
have been granted protection by an immigration judge"
when the decision was being appealed by the government.[208] However, the new parole directive issued by ICE in
November 2007 rescinded prior parole guidelines—
including this guidance.[209]

Even when ICE is not appealing an immigration judge's
ruling, some refugees and other immigrants who have
been found eligible for other forms of protection have been
detained for several additional months. For example, some
individuals who were granted relief under the Convention
Against Torture—because they had shown that they were
more likely than not to be victims of torture if returned to
their home countries—were detained by ICE for an
additional 90 days even after the judge granted them
relief. Attorneys in Arizona, Florida, Illinois, Michigan, and
Minnesota report that this is "often" the case in their
areas. In Arizona and Florida, individuals who were
determined by the U.S. to be "refugees" and were granted
"withholding of removal"—and who therefore cannot be
returned to the country in which they fear persecution—
have also sometimes been detained for up to an
additional 90 days.[210]

Pro bono attorneys in Arizona and Florida report that local
ICE officials have advised them that these individuals are
being detained during this time under a regulation that

allows ICE to identify a "third country" for possible
deportation—a country other than the individual's country
of origin that would be willing to accept the individual.[211]
Attorneys reported that they had no indication from ICE
that it was actively searching out realistic alternatives for
deportation in these cases.

Statistics on Detention and Parole of Asylum Seekers

In 1999, Congress passed a law requiring U.S. immigration authorities to provide statistics on the detention and
parole of asylum seekers to Congress on an annual basis,
and to the public whenever requested.[212] Under this law,
annual reports must be submitted to Congress containing
information on the number of asylum seekers detained,
the detention facilities where they are held, the average
length of detention, and the rate of release for each
immigration district.

ICE has not provided to Congress these Congressionally-
mandated reports on the detention of asylum seekers for
fiscal year 2005. ICE has also not yet released statistics
for fiscal year 2008, which ended on September 30,
2008. Moreover, the figures that ICE has provided for
2006 may be inaccurate (or at least unclear) in part as
they appear to indicate in one place (though not in
another) that only 257 "credible fear" asylum seekers—
rather than over 3,300—were detained during the year.[213]
Not only should these statistics be provided on a more
timely basis, but their accuracy also needs to be
improved. For example, these statistics end up understat-
ing the average length of detention for asylum seekers
since the averages presented do not include (1) longer
term detentions of asylum seekers who are still detained
at the time the statistics are generated, or (2) longer term
detention of asylum seekers detained in previous years
who continue to remain in detention. ICE also does not

appear to have any way of knowing the exact number of asylum seekers who are detained at any one point in time.[214]

Human Rights First has made two requests to ICE under the Freedom of Information Act to obtain statistics and other information on the detention of asylum seekers in recent years. The first FOIA request, filed in June 2006, was initially denied. ICE reversed its decision in November 2008 following an appeal filed by Human Rights First in January 2008, but has yet to produce any data on the detention of asylum seekers in fiscal years 2005, and provided statistics for 2007 to Human Rights First immediately prior to the release of this report. A second FOIA request—for more recent statistics on the detention of asylum seekers as well as for information on the consideration of the availability of legal, medical, and other resources prior to opening new detention facilities—was filed in the summer of 2008 and Human Rights First was still awaiting the production of documents in June 2009.

The Impact of Detention

"Sometimes I just cried, cried, cried... I cried because I had no family, nobody to take care of me, I didn't know how to get a lawyer."

Refugee from Liberia who spent five months in U.S. immigration detention before being granted asylum

"A [detention facility] officer took me to processing. They asked me about my medical situation. They gave me a uniform. You're always worried because you're going to be held in detention, you don't know how long you will be there, don't know what will happen to you next, you have lost connection with your family. It adds on to the stress—you've had bad experiences being imprisoned before. In detention you're treated like illegal human beings."

Guinean human rights defender who had been jailed by Guinean security forces due to his human rights work, and was then detained at the Elizabeth Detention Center in New Jersey for four months

Detention negatively affects the mental health of asylum seekers, and their poor psychological health deteriorates further the longer they remain in detention. Detention also undermines the ability of refugees to win asylum—by making it more difficult for them to obtain legal representation and limiting their ability to gather information in support of their asylum requests. Some refugees may even decide to abandon their requests for asylum in the United States, because they cannot bear to be detained any longer in a U.S. immigration jail.

Increased Trauma and Depression

"Anyone can understand the pain I was going through in jail. I had left my family far away, had asked for asylum, and then I was put in jail. Sometimes I felt like just breaking down and crying, but I did my best to stay strong."

Refugee from Somalia detained at the Otay Mesa detention center in San Diego for four months before being granted asylum by the immigration judge

In reports and assessments released over the last six years, medical and mental health experts have documented the harmful impact of detention on the physical and mental health of asylum seekers. Physicians for Human Rights (PHR) and the Bellevue/NYU Program for Survivors of Torture issued a comprehensive report in June 2003 that concluded that the detention of asylum seekers inflicts further harm on what is an already traumatized population.[215] The 70 participants in the study were asylum seekers confined in detention facilities and jails in New Jersey, New York, and Pennsylvania, with the majority of detained asylum seekers who were interviewed coming from countries in Africa.[216] The average length of detention at the time of the interviews was five months, with a range that stretched from one month to five years.[217] The study found that detained asylum seekers suffer extreme y high levels of anxiety, depression, and Post Traumatic Stress Disorder (PTSD). Specifically, it found that of those interviewed:

- 86 percent suffered from significant depression;

- 77 percent suffered from anxiety; and

- 50 percent suffered from PTSD.[218]

Moreover, the study found that the already poor psychological health of asylum seekers worsened the longer they remained in custody. In fact, uncertainty about the length of detention was itself a significant cause of anxiety and mental distress.[219] Given the impact of detention, the PHR/Bellevue report recommended that asylum seekers who are not a flight or security risk be released on parole. The report also recommended that asylum seekers who are not eligible for unconditional parole be released from detention and placed into alternatives to detention programs. The medical experts specifically recommended that asylum seekers not be shackled, be permitted to wear personal clothing, be allowed more liberal visitation by friends, family and others, and be provided with adequate medical and mental health services.[220]

Numerous other studies have also confirmed that detention has a negative and sometimes lasting impact on the mental health of asylum seekers.[221] For example, a 2006 study on the effects of detention on asylum seekers in Australia concluded that "prolonged detention exerts a long-term impact on the psychological well-being of refugees." The study also documented that the negative mental health effects of detention on asylum seekers "persist for a prolonged period after detention."[222]

The psychological health of detained asylum seekers worsens the longer they remain in detention.

Two years after the release of the PHR/Bellevue report, the U.S. Commission on International Religious Freedom concluded that detention in prison-like facilities was not appropriate for asylum seekers. The Commission's expert on detention conditions reported that "the painful and traumatic aspects of detention...will represent a form of 're-traumatization'" for asylum seekers—who have often been victims of trauma, including torture, imprisonment and other kinds of abuse.[223]

Impact on Ability to Win Asylum

The U.S. government does not provide funding for legal representation of asylum seekers and other immigrants.[224] For those who cannot afford to pay for counsel, the availability of free legal assistance is limited. The need for representation far exceeds the limited resources of nonprofit legal organizations. In fact, in fiscal year 2008, more than a third of detained asylum seekers were not represented at their asylum hearing, and in some locations the rate of unrepresented detained asylum seekers is 60 percent or more.[225] (U.S. immigration courts granted about 45 percent of asylum requests in fiscal year 2008.) Studies on representation of asylum seekers have consistently found that representation is the single most important factor in whether the individual will be granted asylum. A 2007 study found that represented asylum seekers were almost three times as likely to be granted asylum as those without legal representation.[226] Detention, however, restricts an asylum seeker's ability to obtain legal representation. Detained asylum seekers are much less likely to secure legal representation according to U.S. government statistics. More than a third of detained asylum seekers remain unrepresented, but more than 80 percent of non-detained asylum seekers have representation.[227] The Vera Institute for Justice, in a May 2008 report, also found that asylum seekers who received legal orientation presentations while in detention were much more likely to be represented if they were released from detention.[228]

Detained asylum seekers also face greater hurdles in preparing and presenting their cases. Seeking asylum is an intricate process. An asylum seeker's ability to play an active role in his or her case—by gathering evidence, contacting potential witnesses, or conducting legal research if not represented—is severely undermined by detention.[229] In addition, detained asylum seekers often have little or no meaningful access to up-to-date legal materials and country condition reports that are essential to the preparation of their cases.[230]

Access to a phone is crucial in obtaining an attorney, particularly for those detainees who do not receive legal orientation presentations or regular visitors. And for those who do have counsel, phone access is essential for communicating with counsel and assisting the attorney in preparing the case. According to the ICE Detention Standards, all facilities "shall enable all detainees to make calls to the [EOIR]-provided list of free legal service providers and consulates at no charge to the detainee or the receiving party."[231] At many of its facilities, ICE contracts with a private company to provide a *pro bono* telephone system to allow detainees to contact consulates and *pro bono* organizations free of charge. Despite this arrangement, a July 2007 report by the Government Accountability Office (GAO) found "systematic problems" with the *pro bono* telephone system at 16 of the 17 detention centers it inspected. The GAO also concluded that the system was "cumbersome and complicated to use."[232]

During a tour of the South Texas Detention Center organized by Human Rights First, an attorney who worked for a local *pro bono* organization attempted to place a call to her office. She was required to go through multiple steps before being able to place the call, and was only able to get through to her office with the assistance of one of the facility's staff. The data reviewed by the GAO for its report found that, over a five year period, 41 percent of calls placed through the system were not successful.[233] In addition, the telephones are routinely located in large "pod" areas that may hold dozens of other detainees, so that no meaningful degree of privacy is available to make confidential calls to legal counsel or potential witnesses.[234]

Asylum seekers and other immigrant detainees have reported to Human Rights First that the charges for calls are extremely high—an expense that can hinder a detainee's ability to keep in regular contact with his or her attorney and family members. The GAO report found that the charges for international calls ranged between $0.65 and $0.95 per minute at ICE-run and contract facilities, and could be much higher at local jails.[235] In response to similar complaints and in an effort to provide a more cost-effective alternative, the Piedmont Regional Jail in Virginia installed regular payphones in the cells holding immigration detainees.

Driven to Abandon Protection

Because detention can be particularly difficult for victims of persecution and torture, some asylum seekers may decide to withdraw their applications and return to their home country—even though they would face grave danger there—rather than face the prospect of months of additional detention in the United States as their cases make their way through the system. Others give up efforts to block their deportation while their cases are on appeal. The U.S. Commission on International Religious Freedom's study documented a number of instances in which asylum seekers cited harsh detention conditions as a factor in the decision to abandon their asylum claims. The study concluded that some asylum seekers who may very well be eligible for asylum "could be deterred from continuing to pursue their claims because they are forced to remain in detention throughout the course of the asylum process." For arriving asylum seekers in particular, many expressed surprise at being handcuffed, imprisoned and treated like criminals when they came to the United States to flee persecution and seek protection. [236]

Through its interviews with asylum seekers and their attorneys, as well as through its own *pro bono* representation work, Human Rights First has learned of cases of asylum seekers who decided to abandon their cases or stop fighting their deportation rather than spend more time detained in U.S. immigration jails. For example:

A young woman from Brazil escaped brutal domestic violence, and was detained in Florida upon arrival in the United States. Her pro bono attorney filed two parole applications with ICE requesting that her client be released from detention: one in February and a second one in April 2008. The attorney provided proof that a local women's shelter was willing to sponsor the young woman. The request was also accompanied by a five page affidavit from a mental health professional detailing the hardships the young woman had suffered and the difficulties she was encountering in coping with her detention. The first request remained unanswered, and the second request was denied by ICE. The denial stated that the young woman had failed to show that she fell in one of the described parole categories—serious medical condition, pregnant women, juveniles, government witnesses, or parole being in the public interest. The young woman's asylum claim was not successful before the immigration judge. Though her attorney believed her client's chances of winning on appeal were strong, the asylum seeker could not cope with any additional time in detention and chose to forego the appeal and let ICE return her to Brazil despite her fears of harm there.[237]

A 19-year-old woman from Colombia was abducted twice by members of the Revolutionary Armed Forces of Colombia (FARC)—a leftist guerilla insurgent group—as a result of her association with military officers and policemen. After a third kidnapping in 2006, the young woman fled Colombia and flew to the U.S. in search of refuge. She arrived at Newark Liberty International airport, where she was arrested and detained in New Jersey. Though the immigration judge found her testimony credible, the judge concluded that she had failed to establish that the reason for her persecution fell within the definition of a refugee. A *highly trained psychiatrist who interviewed her concluded that she suffered from anxiety and depression, and that the condition was aggravated by her detention. A request for her release on parole, filed in January 2007 by her pro bono attorneys, never received a response from ICE. In January 2008—after 17 and a half months in detention—the young woman decided that she could no longer cope with the stress of detention, and decided to accept deportation. After her deportation, the Court of Appeals issued a deci-sion finding that the young woman had a well-founded fear of future persecution. The court noted that the refugee had "averred that despite the fact that her 'fear of persecution is as strong as ever[,]' the detention was, in her words, 'affect-ing me physically and destroying me mentally' and suggested that her detention in the United States served as a daily and unwelcome reminder of the indignity of detention at the hands of the FARC."*[238]

Cost of Detention

While detention averages $95 per day, alternatives to detention range from $10 to $14 a day, and release through parole has no financial cost each day.

Since 2005, ICE has increased the number of "beds" it uses to detain immigrants by 78 percent.[239] In the past four years, Congress has doubled the annual budget for ICE detention and removal operations to a current budget of $2.4 billion. Nearly 70 percent—or $1.7 billion—is devoted to "custody operations."[240] In fiscal year 2007 alone, ICE detained over 310,000 asylum seekers and immigrants,[241] and in fiscal year 2009, ICE planned to detain over 440,000.[242]

ICE does not provide detailed information about the specific costs of detaining asylum seekers. However, as detailed below, Human Rights First has calculated some of the costs of detaining asylum seekers using various government statistics. For example, as detailed below, ICE has spent:

- More than $300 million to detain asylum seekers from March 2003—when ICE assumed immigration responsibilities—to February 2009.

- More than $12 million to detain over 2,000 asylum seekers at a Texas detention facility during 2007, and over $1 million to detain the last 40 refugees represented by Human Rights First at a detention center in New Jersey.

- About $20,000 to detain a Tibetan refugee for eight months in a California jail, and $25,000 to detain a Somali woman for over five months. They were both subsequently granted asylum.

While ICE pays $95 a day on average to detain an asylum seeker or other immigration detainee, supervised release programs and other alternatives to detention cost much less—$10 to $14 a day. Release on parole incurs no additional cost.

Cost of Detaining Asylum Seekers

Based on various reports and statistics that have been provided by ICE and by U.S. Citizenship and Immigration Services, Human Rights First has calculated that ICE has spent somewhere over **$300 million to detain over 48,000 asylum seekers** from March 2003 to February 2009.[243] The costs are actually likely higher since this number does not include all categories of asylum seekers detained in 2005 and from October 2007 through early 2009 (ICE has not provided reports for these periods yet). Moreover, this number is based on ICE statistics concerning average detention lengths which do not reflect longer term detentions, as they only track asylum seekers who have been released from detention and not those who were still detained when the statistics were generated.[244] In fiscal year 2007 alone, ICE reported that it detained **9,971 asylum seekers** for an average detention period of nearly two and a half months—though the average length of detention was likely greater, again because the average did not include long term detentions. The cost of detaining these asylum seekers, Human Rights First has calculated, was about **$88.8 million**.[245] This cost may also be higher, as the average detention period did not reflect longer term detentions.

According to information provided to Human Rights First by ICE, more than **2,000 asylum seekers,** detained under the expedited removal and credible fear process, were detained at the Pearsall detention facility in Texas during 2007, each for an average of 75 days. At an average cost of detention of $84.51 per day at the facility, Human Rights First has calculated that the **detention of these asylum seekers cost more than $12 million**.

The cost of detention varies by facility. The Elizabeth Detention Center in New Jersey, for example has a daily detention cost of $161.42.[246] The average length of detention for Human Rights First's last 40 refugee clients detained at the facility—who were found to be refugees deserving of protection by U.S. immigration authorities—was between five and six months. The average cost of detaining these refugees was therefore about $25,000 to $29,000 each, for a total of more than $1 million.

The following chart highlights the cost of detaining asylum seekers at select detention facilities:

Detention facility	Cost per day	Asylum seekers detained in FY 2006*[247]	Estimated cost of detention (based on average length of detention of 71.5 days, as last reported by ICE in 2004)[248]
Suffolk County (Mass.)	$90[249]	84	$540,540
San Diego Correctional Facility (Cal.)	$89.50[250]	369	$2,361,323.25
Piedmont Regional Jail (Va.)	$46.25[251]	45	$148,809.38
South Texas (Pearsall) Detention Center (Tex.)	$84.51[252]	501	$3,027,274.97
Elizabeth Detention Center (N.J.)	$161.42[253]	285	$3,289,226.05
Yuba County Jail (Cal.)	$71.58[254]	186	$951,942.42
TOTAL		**1,470**	**$10,319,116.07**

* Does not include asylum seekers detained in previous years and in continued detention during FY 2006. Furthermore, this statistical report provided by ICE may under-report the number of detained arriving asylum seekers.

In addition, Human Rights First has also calculated (next page) the cost of detaining some of the individual refugees we have represented or interviewed. We've also estimated the cost savings to ICE if these individuals had been released on parole after two weeks, or to an "alternatives to detention" program. For example:

- The detention of an **Iraqi Christian refugee,** who was detained at the Otay Mesa facility in San Diego for four and a half months, cost ICE at least $89.50 per night, for a total **detention cost of more than $12,000**. If instead he had been released on parole after two weeks in detention, the cost would have been closer to $1,250, and if he had been released to an alternatives-to-detention program, the costs would have been only about $2,000–$10,000 less than detention.[255]

- The detention of a **Burmese Baptist Chin woman,** who spent more than two years detained at the El Paso Service Processing Center (an ICE-managed detention center, with the average daily cost of detention at ICE-run facilities at $119.28[256]) **cost more than $90,000**. If instead, she had been released on parole after two weeks in detention, the cost would have been closer to $1,670, and if she had been released to an alternatives-to-detention program, the costs would have been closer to $7,630 to $10,680.[257]

- The detention of a Tibetan refugee for **eight months** at the Santa Ana jail in California cost **$19,680 at $82 per night**.[258] If instead he had been released on parole after two weeks in detention, the cost would have been closer to $1,148, and if he had been released to an alternatives-to-detention program, the costs would have been closer to $2,400 to $3,360.[259]

- The detention of a woman from Somalia who was detained at the Elizabeth Detention Center in New Jersey for **more than five months** until she was granted asylum, cost **$161.42 per night for a total of $25,827.20**. If instead, she had been released on parole after two weeks in detention, the cost would have been closer to $2,260, and if she had been released to an alternatives-to-detention program, the

costs would have been closer to $1,600 to $2,240.[260]

- The detention of a Burmese refugee at the Pearsall Detention Center, who was **detained for seven months, cost more than $17,700 at $84.51 per night**. If instead, she had been released on parole after two weeks in detention, the cost would have been closer to $1,180, and if she had been released to an alternatives-to-detention program, the costs would have been closer to $2,100 to $2,940.[261]

Cost Savings Through Release on Parole or Alternatives to Detention

While detention costs $95 a day, alternatives to detention cost between $10 and $14 per day depending on the program and its location according to ICE statistics.[262] The release of an asylum seeker on parole or on a bond, when appropriate (i.e., when they satisfy the criteria for release), has essentially no daily financial cost to ICE. If an asylum seeker were released on parole after an initial detention period of two weeks, the costs of detention could be significantly reduced from several thousand dollars and sometimes tens of thousands of dollars to about $1,330.[263]

Where some additional supervision is determined to be necessary, an individual may be able to be released to an "alternatives to detention" program. (See "Alternatives to Detention or Alternatives to Release?" below.) These kinds of programs include various kinds of monitoring mechanisms, such as telephone reporting, in-person check-ins, curfews and—in their most restrictive form—an electronic monitoring device (often called an "ankle bracelet"). While the average cost of detaining an asylum seeker for three months is $8,730, the cost to ICE if the asylum seeker is instead released into an alternatives-to-detention program for the same time period is only $900 to $1,260. And even if the case were to take twice as long once the asylum seeker is released into an alternatives-to-detention program, the cost savings would still be substantial at more than $6,000.[264] The Vera Institute of Justice concluded that the cost of supervising release was 55 percent less than the cost of detention.[265]

Medical and Mental Health Care Deficiencies

"Immediately my body started shaking. I felt so cold that I thought I was freezing to death, but at the same time I was sweating...Within minutes I had a seizure and my body began to shake so violently that I fell off the bed onto the floor... At the hospital, I had my stomach pumped so that I would throw up the medication that was inside me... I was then taken back to the detention center. The next day I was still feeling sick. I was vomiting continuously. I lost control of myself and fainted... They gave me an I.V. and I started bleeding from my mouth and my private parts... The examining doctor came and informed me that the test results showed damage to my liver... It took about a month for me to feel better."

Testimony before the House Subcommittee on Homeland Security of a refugee woman from Ethiopia who was detained for five months at the San Pedro Processing Center in California, and was mistakenly given medication by a nurse—without the use of an interpreter—that had not been prescribed to her, June 2008

Over the last year, a number of U.S. government assessments, media reports and other studies have identified serious deficiencies in the health care provided to asylum seekers and immigrants who are held in detention centers and jails across the country.[266] These reports have documented a range of problems, including:

- Severe staffing shortages, with over 140 medical staff openings and an 18 percent vacancy rate for medical staff as of June 2008;[267]

- Failures to use interpreters to communicate with detainees during medical exams, in some cases leading to dangerous misdiagnoses, and[268]

- 90 deaths of detainees since ICE's inception in 2003, including 13 suicides.[269]

In addition, these reports have detailed failures by medical staff to administer mandatory physical exams that are required to take place within 24 hours of detention, as well as initial medical screenings.[270] The reports have also documented examples of significant delays and backlogs in responding to detainee requests for medical attention.[271]

Medical Staffing Shortages at Detention Facilities

"Documents tell us that employees widely complained of severe staffing shortages of medical personnel. ICE tells us they are addressing these shortages now, but the documents indicate they ignored these warnings for years, failing to adequately address these shortages even as they ramped up enforcement and brought detention beds on line."

Zoe Lofgren, Chairwoman of House Judiciary Subcommittee on Immigration, Citizenship, Refugees, Border Security, and International Law, Hearing on Problems with Immigration Detainee Medical Care, June 4, 2008

The capacity to provide medical care to detainees has not kept up with the steep rise in the number of detention beds, which have increased by 78 percent since fiscal year 2005.[272] The Division of Immigration Health Services (DIHS), which provides medical care at all facilities operated by ICE or private contractors, has experienced severe staffing shortages. Though DHS officials testified before Congress in June 2008 that they were actively working to reduce the number of unfilled positions, the vacancy rate at the time of the hearing was still at 18 percent.[273]

Staffing shortages have been exacerbated by ICE's decision to detain asylum seekers and other immigrants at facilities that are not located in areas that would have a pool of medical professionals available. During Human Rights First's visit to the South Texas Detention Center in May 2008, the medical staff was unable to tell us how many vacancies they had, but we were informed that the DIHS was trying to fill positions for a physician, a physician's assistant, a nurse practitioner, a dentist, and several nurses. The facility is located in the town of Pearsall (population 7,157), 135 miles from Austin and 57 miles from San Antonio. DHS's Office of Inspector General reported that at the time of its visit in October 2007, Pearsall had 22 medical staff vacancies, and that "[g]iven its rural location and the nation's high demand for nurses, staff in Pearsall said that they will endure medical staff shortages indefinitely."[274] As preparations were under way to open the new 1,162-bed detention facility in Jena, Louisiana, the then-interim director of DIHS wrote to ICE expressing his concerns that DIHS was "facing critical staffing shortages at most every other DIHS site" and they had "been unable to meet the demand."[275] The Jena facility, opened in November 2007, is located 140 miles from Baton Rouge and 228 miles from New Orleans. ICE has continued to detain asylum seekers and other immigrants at the Pearsall and Jena facilities despite these concerns.

At the June 4, 2008, Congressional hearing, then-ICE Assistant Secretary Julie Myers admitted that there were concerns with regard to staffing shortages and testified that ICE had "reduced the staffing issues from 30 percent vacancies down to 18."[276] A Human Rights First review of job postings on DIHS's website confirmed that the agency was still hiring to fill 137 medical positions as of the end of March 2009, including twelve at the Pearsall detention center and seven at the Jena detention center—including a clinical director and staff physician at each of the facilities.[277]

Lack of Interpretation

"I didn't have an interpreter when they took me to the medical clinic. My English is not too correct, but I tried to explain that my stomach is hurting. I took my hand and put it on my stomach, and they gave me medicine."

Refugee woman from Liberia who was detained for five months in New Jersey

Asylum seekers in U.S. immigration jails come from a wide range of countries and speak languages that include Amharic, Burmese, Creole, French, Fulani, Mandingo, Pushtu, Russian, Somali, Spanish, and Tibetan. The ICE Detention Standards state that if "language difficulties prevent the health care provider/officer from sufficiently communicating with the detainee for purposes of completing the medical screening, the officer *shall* obtain translation assistance" [emphasis added].[273] Of the asylum seekers Human Rights First interviewed for this report, several reported that medical staff did not obtain an interpreter when providing medical care. In a 2003 report, Physicians for Human Rights and the NYU/Bellevue Center for Survivors of Torture reported that 37 percent of the asylum seekers they interviewed had not been provided an interpreter or had a lot of difficulty securing one for the purposes of obtaining medical care.[279]

ICE has no system in place to track when an interpreter is used for purposes of providing medical care. At some facilities, medical personnel will sometimes rely on ICE officers or the facility's guards for interpretation.[280] Though all medical personnel—at ICE facilities, contract facilities, and local jails—have access to a telephonic interpretation system, there is no system in place to ensure that asylum seekers are notified of their right to an interpreter and receive one when needed.

A refugee from Somalia, Amina, was detained at a New Jersey detention center after arriving in the U.S. and requesting protection. Anxious and exhausted, she fainted shortly after being brought to the immigration jail. A doctor employed by the Division of Immigration Health Services examined Amina and misdiagnosed her as being psychotic. The doctor prescribed a strong anti-psychotic drug. The medical staff failed to use an interpreter to communicate with Amina, and Amina did not at first understand what medication she had been prescribed. She also did not have access to her medical records.

Amina secured pro bono counsel through Human Rights First's asylum representation program. Two outside doctors, retained by Amina's pro bono attorney, described the effect that these drugs had on her: "The drug...caused her to experience devastating and life-threatening side effects. [She] began to shake uncontrollably... She vomited regularly... She became dizzy, disoriented and confused. She had difficulty walking, and sometimes fell off her chair."[281] Reflecting on her experience, Amina said, "The medicine made me sick. I feel dizzy all the time. I'm confused."[282] The attorney repeatedly contacted medical officers at the facility to express concerns about the medical treatment her client was receiving. The attorney even offered on repeated occasions to make an interpreter available during Amina's medical visits—at no cost to DIHS or ICE. DIHS continued to examine Amina and provide her with medication without the help of an interpreter. At the advice of the doctor retained by her pro bono attorney—who determined that Amina did not suffer from a psychotic illness—Amina stopped taking the medication.

While in detention, Amina also experienced severe abdominal pain. Her attorney wrote letters to medical staff and called both ICE and medical staff repeatedly. Weeks of constant advocacy went by before Amina received meaningful medical attention. She was only brought to the hospital the day after her pro bono attorney threatened to file a habeas petition in federal court.[283]

Detainee Deaths

ICE took over responsibility for immigration detention six years ago in March 2003. During this time, 90 immigrant detainees have died while in immigration custody,[284] including at least 10 in fiscal year 2008 alone.[285] ICE officials initially stated that the mortality rate for immigra-tion detainees had fallen over the years, and have argued that the number of detainee deaths is low when compared to the death rate among criminal prisoners.[286] A physician from the Bellevue/New York University Program for Survivors of Torture testified in June 2008 before the House Judiciary Subcommittee on Immigration that—taking into account the length of detention of immigration detainees—the mortality of immigrants in detention actually increased by 29 percent between fiscal years 2006 and 2007.[287] He also noted that comparisons between the ICE detainee population and the general criminal prison population are inadequate, since criminal prisoners are typically held for longer periods of time on average and have different risk factors. A Government Accountability Office report, published in February 2009, concluded that ICE's mortality rate cannot be directly compared to that of other prisoners "due to differences in the agencies' health care goals, scopes of service, and population demographics."[288]

More than a dozen of the documented deaths since 2003 have been suicides. At a June 2008 oversight hearing, the then-Assistant Secretary of ICE, Julie Myers, testified that

there had been no reported suicides in the previous 15 months.[289] No suicides have been publicly reported since June 2008. The Director of ICE's Office of Detention and Removal Operations, James T. Hayes, Jr., stated at a March 2009 Congressional hearing that the Department of Homeland Security would begin requiring the release of the number of immigration detainees who die in custody to the Department of Justice beginning in 2009.[290]

Mental Health Care Needs of Survivors of Torture

Asylum seekers who are detained in U.S. immigration jails suffer from high levels of depression, anxiety and post-traumatic stress disorder, and these conditions worsen the longer they are detained, according to a study conducted by Physicians for Human Rights and the Bellevue/NYU Program for Survivors of Torture.[291] Some asylum seekers are survivors of torture and may still be suffering from the psychological effects of that torture. But specialized counseling and other support mechanisms are either not available or very limited for asylum seekers who are held in immigration detention. At the same time, asylum seekers and other immigrant detainees have reported difficulties in obtaining adequate mental health care more broadly, as docu-mented in a number of recent reports.[292]

Isolated Facilities and Access to Justice

As DHS and ICE have expanded immigration detention over the last few years, they have repeatedly chosen to detain asylum seekers and immigrants in new facilities that are located in areas that are not near *pro bono* legal resources, the immigration courts, or U.S. asylum offices. For example, between 2005 and 2008 alone, ICE began detaining immigrants and asylum seekers at the:

■ **Willacy Detention Center**: Located in Raymondville, Texas, the facility—which, with its 3,000 beds s the largest U.S. immigration detention center—is 230 miles from San Antonio and 300 miles from Austin.

■ **Stewart Detention Center**: Located in Lumpkin, Georgia, the 1,524-bed facility is 140 miles south of Atlanta, where the immigration courts and some *pro bono* legal resources are located.

■ **Otero County Processing Center**: Located in Chaparral, New Mexico, this 1,088-bed facility is 22 miles outside El Paso, Texas, where the nearest *pro bono* legal organizations—which are already over-stretched trying to assist asylum seekers and immigrants at the El Paso facility—are located.

■ **South Texas (Pearsall) Detention Center**: Located in Pearsall, Texas (population 7,157), the 1,904-bed facility is 57 miles outside of San Antonio and 135 miles south of Austin, the nearest hub of *pro bono* legal service providers. The facility is a four-hour drive from the Houston asylum office, which is responsible for conducting credible fear screening interviews for asylum seekers detained at the facility.

■ **LaSalle (Jena) Detention Center**: Located in Jena, Louisiana, this 1,162-bed facility is 140 miles from Baton Rouge and 228 miles from New Orleans, where *pro bono* legal resources are located.

■ **McHenry County Jail**: Located in Woodstock, Illinois, the jail—with about 200 beds contracted by ICE—is more than 60 miles from Chicago, the nearest hub of *pro bono* legal service providers and where the immigration court is located.

According to ICE, detention facilities "are strategically placed to support immigration law enforcement programs and/or to facilitate easier removal of detainees to Central American countries."[293] The rate charged by contractors to detain asylum seekers and other immigrants at some of these remote facilities may also be less than the rate charged at more central locations.[294] However, detention at remote facilities leads to other government costs, such as transfers and the additional costs that would be incurred by the immigration courts or the USCIS asylum office to transport judges and asylum officers to and from these facilities.[295]

Detention in a remote area can compound the difficulty of finding and retaining competent staffing. After a visit to the South Texas Detention Center, for example, the DHS Office of Inspector General noted that staff at the facility believed staff vacancies in the medical department would endure "indefinitely" due to the facility's "rural location."[296]

As detailed below, asylum seekers who have been detained at these remote facilities have faced a series of challenges. In too many instances, facilities used by ICE were opened for months or even years before a Legal Orientation Program was put in place to provide basic legal information to detainees—a decision which left hundreds of asylum seekers and other immigrant detainees without basic legal information and counseling to help them navigate the system and obtain legal representation. These remote locations have also undermined the access of asylum seekers to legal orientation presentations and to legal representation itself. At the same time, asylum seekers and other immigrant detainees increasingly see immigration judges and U.S. asylum officers on television screens due to the use of video conferencing for hearings and credible fear interviews.

Legal Orientation Presentations

The Department of Justice has contracted with the Vera Institute of Justice since 2003 to provide legal presentations to immigration detainees in some—but not all—areas with low rates of representation and limited legal services. Known as the Legal Orientation Program (LOP), these legal presentations are conducted by nongovernmental organizations, and provide both group orientations as well as a limited number of individual workshops. In addition to the Department of Justice's program, nongovernmental organizations around the country have also coordinated legal orientation presentations at detention facilities in their areas. For example, Human Rights First works with other local nongovernmental organizations to provide legal orientation presentations to detainees at the Elizabeth Detention Center in New Jersey.

Providing basic information about the asylum process, the law on eligibility for asylum, and the availability of legal services to detained asylum seekers is an important initial step in ensuring that asylum seekers have a meaningful opportunity to request protection. A study released in May 2008 by the Vera Institute—as part of the program performance evaluation required by its contract with the Department of Justice—concluded that unrepresented

asylum seekers were more likely to be granted asylum when they received individual orientations in addition to group orientations. Specifically, the study found that asylum seekers who had received more intensive services were granted relief at a higher rate than those asylum seekers who only attended the group orientations.[297] Asylum seekers who have actual legal representation are granted asylum at higher rates.[298]

However, as the Vera study documented, "the expansion of detention has outpaced the expansion of funding for the Legal Orientation Program."[299] In 2007, for example, the program provided presentations to 34,000 detainees—just over 10 percent of all individuals detained during that period.[300] In fiscal year 2008, $3.76 million was appropriated to fund the Legal Orientation Program. This enabled the program to reach 48,000 detained immigrants and asylum seekers. During fiscal year 2009, $4 million—only a slight increase from the previous year—was appropriated for the Legal Orientation Program. According to ICE, more than 440,000 immigrants will be detained during 2009 at several hundred facilities.[301] In late 2008, the Legal Orientation Program was expanded to twelve new locations, including to the Willacy detention center—the "Tent City"—in Raymondville, Texas. These legal presentations are now operational at 25 detention facilities,[302] but they still will only reach approximately 11 percent of detained immigrants and asylum seekers.[303]

Several of the mega-facilities opened by ICE in the past few years were open for months or even years before a Legal Orientation Program was put in place. The South Texas (Pearsall) Detention Center, which opened its doors in May 2005, did not have legal orientation presentations in place until October 2006—well over a year after it opened. Here are a few examples:

Detention Facility	Date opened	LOP start date	Time facility was opened without LOP
Willacy Detention Center	July 2006	November 2008	2 ½ years
Otay Mesa Detention Facility	2000	February 2008	8 years
South Texas Detention Center	May 2005	October 2006	1 year +
Stewart Detention Center	October 2006	November 2008	2 years
Jena Detention Facility	November 2007	December 2008	1 year

As a result, hundreds of asylum seekers and immigrant detainees were detained at facilities without access to a legal presentation to help them find legal representation or to provide them with basic information about the system and their options. Many may have abandoned their cases or were unable to win without this assistance.

Religious and Spiritual Support

In addition to detaining asylum seekers and other immigrants at facilities that do not have adequate legal support services in place, ICE has also detained immigrants at facilities that do not have adequate religious and spiritual support programs in place.

The spiritual programs at the seven ICE-run Service Processing Centers are staffed through a contract with Church World Service Religious Services Program. Through Church World Service, each detention center has two staff members who work in the facility plus an administrative staff member who provides off-site support. In addition, Church World Service is able to draw on dozens of community volunteers to provide proper religious services for detainees of any faith.

However, many other facilities, including contract facilities and county jails, do not have this kind of support. The Willacy Detention Center—now expanded to 3,000 beds—for example, had only one chaplain and no assistant at the time of Human Rights First's visit in May 2008, and this was still the case in March 2009.[304] Similarly, the 1,904-bed Pearsall Detention Center also had only one chaplain at the time of Human Rights First's visit in May 2008.

Asylum seekers and other immigrants have also been detained in county and local jails that do not have legal orientation presentations in place. For example, during the spring of 2006, ICE began sending asylum seekers and other detainees to the Regional Correctional Center (RCC) in Albuquerque, New Mexico—a facility that did not have legal presentations in place and was not located near existing legal resources for immigrants. Asylum seekers from China and Cuba were reported to be among those transferred to this local jail. Legal presentations did not begin at this facility for more than six months after the facility began to be used by ICE. After local legal service providers learned that asylum seekers and other immigrants were being detained at RCC, the Catholic Diocesan Migrant and Refugee Services began organizing monthly group presentations for detainees. ICE withdrew all 600 immigration detainees from the RCC in August 2007, following numerous reports of poor detention conditions.[305]

Access to Legal Representation

"Our Austin office is located more than 100 miles from the Pearsall Detention Center—a facility, located in a remote rural area, where many asylum seekers are held. The four hour roundtrip drive and long waits to see our clients even after we arrive at the facility limit our ability to take on more cases of asylum seekers detained at Pearsall."

Attorney at Catholic Charities of Central Texas, Austin, February 2009[306]

Legal representation is the single most important factor in determining whether an individual will be granted asylum, according to studies on representation of asylum seekers.[307] One study conducted by legal experts found that represented asylum seekers were almost three times as likely to be granted asylum in immigration court than those who were unrepresented.[308] A report by the Government Accountability Office similarly found "more than a three-fold increase" in the asylum grant rate for asylum seekers who were represented, as compared to those without representation.[309]

Despite the quantifiable difference legal representation can make, many asylum seekers do not have a lawyer, and are left to navigate the complex system on their own. Asylum seekers are less likely to obtain legal representa-

tion if they are in immigration detention. Over one-third of detained asylum seekers do not have legal representation in immigration court.[310]

The remote location of some immigration detention facilities increases the difficulty of securing legal representation for asylum seekers. Overstretched and underfunded nonprofit organizations may have little or no capacity to send an attorney—perhaps their only attorney—on a multi-hour trip to a detention facility. During that same time, the organization could have assisted several other immigrants who were not detained. Long wait times at detention centers can also limit legal representation. In addition to the several hours of travel time to and from a facility, some attorneys—like those who represent asylum seekers detained at the Pearsall facility—experience delays in gaining access to their asylum clients after arriving at the facility.[311]

A representative from a San Antonio pro bono legal organization that represents asylum seekers detained at the Pearsall detention center, reported regularly having to wait two or more hours before being able to meet with his clients. On one occasion, he recounted, he waited five hours. Delays are in part due to the fact that the detention facility—though housing nearly 2,000 detainees and about 200 asylum seekers at any given time—only has three attorney-client visitation rooms. Facility staff also informed pro bono attorneys that they did not have sufficient staff to escort detainees to and from the visitation rooms in a timely manner.

In its 2005 study, the U.S. Commission on International Religious Freedom found that many of the facilities used to detain asylum seekers subject to expedited removal were "located in rural parts of the United States, where few lawyers visit and even fewer maintain a practice." The Commission concluded that "[t]he practical effect of detention in remote locations…is to restrict asylum seekers' legally authorized right to counsel."[312] A May

2008 report issued by the Vera Institute of Justice, a nonprofit organization which contracts with the Department of Justice to provide legal orientation presentations at a number of facilities, found that "[a]t several sites, the remote location of the detention facilities...a shortage of mentors for legal representatives without experience in immigration law, and a lack of *pro bono* counsel have all presented significant obstacles" to coordinating *pro bono* representation for detainees.[313]

Remote Detention Locations Limit Representation

In June 2008, a new 1,086-bed immigration detention center opened in Otero County, New Mexico. It is located near the existing Otero County Prison, which holds immigrant detainees. An attorney from a nonprofit legal service provider in El Paso said: "Individuals detained at the Otero Service Processing Center face several challenges. There are few opportunities to receive free legal representation in New Mexico. The closest city to Otero is El Paso, and most of the nonprofit organizations in El Paso receive funding to provide free services to individuals detained in Texas [not New Mexico]. Due to the remote location, even private attorneys are a good distance from Otero. Individuals detained in Otero are often transferred to Otero from locations all over the United States. So, in addition to being isolated and away from legal representation, detainees do not have access to family members to assist in the gathering of documents relevant to their case."

Video Justice? U.S. Immigration Court Hearings and Asylum Interviews Conducted by Video

"If someone's sitting in front of you, he can see your emotion. As you tell your story of what's happened to your family and what's happened to your country he can see your emotion. If you're on TV, maybe he can't see you clearly."

> Refugee from Somalia who was detained for nearly five months at the Pearsall Detention Center before being granted asylum

"I thought it was a problem to do court by video, because sometimes the facial features don't appear in detail."

> Iraqi Christian man who was detained for four and a half months at the Otay Mesa facility in California before being granted asylum

At some of these remote detention centers, asylum seekers often see U.S. immigration judges and asylum officers only on television sets. Asylum hearings and asylum screening interviews are increasingly conducted by "video conferencing"—particularly at remote facilities. At the Pearsall facility in Texas, which housed about 900 asylum seekers in 2007 alone, Human Rights First's delegation was informed by local ICE officers that almost all immigration court hearings and asylum office screening interviews are conducted by video conferencing.[314] Similarly, at the Willacy and Port Isabel facilities in southwest Texas, local *pro bono* and other attorneys report that the majority of all hearings—including the merit hearings in asylum cases—are conducted by video conference. Recently, the San Diego immigration court has also begun conducting video hearings with detainees, including asylum seekers.

At some of the remote detention centers, asylum seekers often see U.S. immigration judges only on television sets.

When visiting both the 1,904-bed Pearsall facility and the now 3,000-bed Willacy facility, Human Rights First's delegation saw courtrooms that were centered around television sets, rather than live immigration judges. From our meetings with local immigration officials, *pro bono* attorneys and asylum seekers, Human Rights First learned that—during these video hearings—the asylum seeker may end up sitting essentially alone in the courtroom in front of the television set, or in some cases next to the government's trial attorney, while the judge sits in a courtroom at another location. If the asylum seeker is represented, his or her attorney must choose whether to sit next to the asylum seeker or whether to appear in person before the judge. One federal appeals court called this kind of choice a "Catch 22"—requiring an attorney to decide between the ability to confer with a client during a hearing and the opportunity to "interact effectively" with the judge and opposing counsel.[315]

By 2004, video conferencing equipment had already been installed in 40 immigration courts and 77 other sites, including detention centers and correctional facilities.[316] By May 2006, the number of immigration courts with videoconferencing capabilities had grown to 47 out of the then-existing 53 immigration courts around the country.[317]

The Executive Office for Immigration Review—the branch of the Department of Justice that oversees all immigration courts—anticipated in 2005 that the use of video conferencing in immigration courts would grow, with the goal of having every immigration court outfitted with video conferencing equipment.[318] A February 2009 National Public Radio story on the use of video conference technology in immigration courts reported that ICE plans to have video conferencing capabilities at all new detention locations.[319]

In recent years, there has also been a significant increase in the number of asylum screening interviews—known as credible fear interviews—that are conducted by video conference. The U.S. asylum office—part of DHS's U.S. Citizenship and Immigration Services—began using video conferencing to conduct credible fear interviews in late 2005. In fiscal year 2007, the U.S. asylum office conducted over 60 percent of all credible fear interviews by video conference. If an asylum seeker does not "pass" this interview or a subsequent review (also increasingly conducted by video), the asylum seeker is not even allowed to file an application for asylum in this country. According to statistics provided by the asylum office for fiscal year 2007, the "pass rate" for credible fear interviews conducted by video conference and those conducted in-person was comparable.[320] Other asylum office statistics show that the credible fear "pass rate" fell from 94 to 59 percent between 2004 and 2008.[321] Video conferencing is primarily conducted by the Houston asylum office which has jurisdiction over all the large facilities in Texas as well as asylum seekers detained in New Mexico, Colorado, and several additional states.[322] The Houston asylum office is now responsible for more than half of all credible fear interviews conducted in the United States.[323] The Miami asylum office also conducts some credible fear interviews by video.[324]

The Executive Office for Immigration Review (EOIR) has praised video conferencing as "beneficial to both Immigration Courts and the alien respondent," stating that video conferencing "saves travel time for Immigration Judges...saves travel costs and improves safety and security."[325] EOIR's lack of funding in recent years—especially as compared to ICE—has been widely reported.[326] EOIR has also asserted that video conference hearings are "as fair and effective as in-person hearings."[327]

However, a 2008 analysis published in the Georgetown Immigration Law Journal and based on immigration court statistics provided by the EOIR for fiscal years 2005 and 2006, demonstrates that asylum seekers are about half as likely to be granted asylum when their cases are heard by video conference rather than in person.[328] In asylum cases, asylum seekers have to recount details of trauma and torture. This kind of testimony is difficult enough for a refugee—but testifying before an adjudicator who appears on a television set, with a translator who is often participating by telephone, makes the entire experience surreal. Research on the use of video for communication, including court testimony, has concluded that the technology "does not effectively convey the full range of nonverbal cues" and "inevitably skews the perceptions of others" by altering nonverbal cues and failing to replicate normal eye contact.[329]

A finding as to the asylum seeker's credibility is central to the claim. Immigration law lays the responsibility of making a credibility assessment on the immigration judge, based on "demeanor, candor, or responsiveness" of the applicant, among other factors.[330] When an asylum seeker appears in person before an immigration judge, the judge has an opportunity to observe the witness. According to the 2008 Georgetown study, video conferencing fails to "sufficiently convey a number of the nuanced nonverbal cues that are inherent in oral communication" and "undermines the [asylum seeker's] ability to make the emotional connection" with the judge.[331] The asylum

seeker "will seem less trustworthy and less credible." A judge's perception of a witness's demeanor may be skewed when the judge is only able to see the asylum seeker on a 27 inch television screen. A federal court, reviewing the use of video conferencing in an asylum hearing, stated that video conferencing rendered it "difficult for a factfinder...to make credibility determinations and to gauge demeanor."[332]

Communication with ICE

While larger facilities often have on-site ICE staff, many of the county jails holding immigrant detainees do not have ICE staff working at the facility on a full-time basis. In fact, detainees rely on visits by ICE officers for communication on the status of their cases. During a visit by Human Rights First staff to two Virginia jails (the Hampton Roads Regional Jail and the Piedmont Regional Jail in November 2008), detained asylum seekers and other immigrants reported that they did not have frequent interactions with ICE officers. Detainees reported that ICE officers visited the facility about once a week, but during those visits they only had the opportunity to meet with a handful of detainees and were unable to answer questions on the status of other detainees' cases. Asylum seekers and other immigrants detained at these two Virginia jails also told Human Rights First that, though they had been provided with the name and a phone number for their deportation officer, they were unable to reach them, and when they left voice messages their phone calls were not returned. An ICE deportation officer accompanying Human Rights First on the tours of the facilities confirmed that ICE officers visit the jails about once or twice a week. However, he declined to provide information—citing "security" concerns—on the number of detained cases each ICE deportation officer managed, or how many deportation officers oversaw the cases of the 200-plus detainees at each of the two jails. Local legal representatives in

Minnesota and Illinois also report that there are no ICE officers working at many of the jails where asylum seekers and other immigrants are held, and ICE officers instead visit the facility.

Alternatives to Detention or Alternatives to Release?

"There should be a presumption against detention. Where there are monitoring mechanisms which can be employed as viable alternatives to detention, such as reporting obligations or guarantor requirements...these should be applied first unless there is evidence to suggest that such an alternative will not be effective in the individual case."

UNHCR Revised Guidelines on Applicable Criteria and Standards Relating to the Detention of Asylum Seekers (February 1999)

A number of programs, known as "alternatives to detention," have been successfully tested in the United States. These programs generally provide for release from immigration detention with some additional measures to monitor the individual after release. These measures can include in-person reporting, reporting by telephone, and home visits by representatives of the organization overseeing the program. The UNHCR, in a comprehensive study of alternatives to detention for asylum seekers, concluded that the factors that influence the effectiveness of an alternatives-to-detention program include: the provision of legal services, ensuring that asylum seekers are informed about their rights and obligations, and screening for family or community ties or using community groups as sponsors.[333]

Participants in these kinds of programs have very high "appearance rates" for their immigration court hearings—ranging from 93 percent to 99 percent.[334] While the average daily cost of detention is $95, the average daily cost for an alternatives-to-detention program falls between $10 and $14.[335] These kinds of programs—when used as

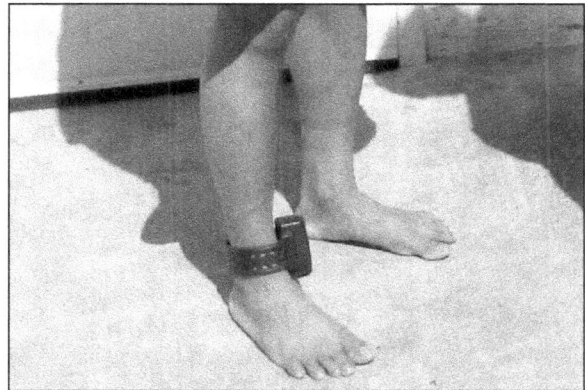

After 30 months in detention and nearly two years of compliance with the alternative program, this Sri Lankan asylum seeker still has to wear a large ankle bracelet.

true alternatives-to-detention for individuals who could not otherwise be released on parole or bond—represent significant cost-savings to the government.

Despite these documented successes and the cost savings of these programs, ICE has not implemented a nationwide program of alternatives to detention for all eligible immigration detainees. Many asylum seekers are never even assessed for potential release through an alternatives-to-detention program. Instead, over the last few years:

- ICE has not requested—and Congress has yet to authorize—sufficient funding to expand alternatives programs and implement them nationwide. Instead of expanding alternatives-to-detention programs—with appearance rates of 93 to 99 percent—for many years, ICE has devoted the overwhelming majority of its growing detention and removal budget to creating more detention beds.[336]

- ICE has relied heavily upon highly restrictive electronic monitoring programs—through the use of "ankle bracelets"—rather than using alternative programs which connect individuals with community-based services, including legal assistance. Such intense monitoring—especially when combined with other forms of supervision such as curfews—can rise to the level of custody, rather than an alternative to custody.

- Instead of using these programs to minimize unnecessary detention of asylum seekers, ICE has used its alternatives-to-detention programs to supervise asylum seekers who would not have previously been detained at all or who would have been released without conditions.

Early Models

A number of successful models of alternatives to detention have been tested in the United States. These early models have demonstrated high appearance rates for asylum seekers—ranging from 93 to 96 percent—with significant cost savings for the U.S. government.

From 1997 to 2000, the Vera Institute of Justice conducted a pilot alternative program. In this pilot program, which was called the Appearance Assistance Program, the Vera Institute supervised the release of asylum seekers and other non-citizens. In order to be released to supervision, participants were required to report regularly in person and by phone. Their whereabouts were monitored. Participants were also provided with information about the consequences of failing to comply with U.S. immigration laws. Participants in a less intensive program were given reminders of court hearings and were provided with legal information, and referrals to lawyers and other services.[337]

The Vera Institute pilot project reported an appearance rate of 93 percent for asylum seekers released through its appearance assistance program, and a saving of almost $4,000 per person. Based on its research, the Vera study concluded, "Asylum seekers do not need to be detained to appear for their hearings. They also do not seem to need intensive supervision."[338]

Another successful alternative model was coordinated by the Lutheran Immigration and Refugee Service (LIRS). Through that project, the former INS released 25 Chinese asylum seekers from detention in Ullin, Illinois, to shelters in several communities. The community shelters reminded participants of their hearings, scheduled check-ins with the INS, organized transportation and accompanied asylum seekers to their appointments. Nonprofit agencies also found *pro bono* attorneys for all of the asylum seekers who were released to the shelters. The project achieved a 96 percent appearance rate.[339]

Current Programs: Limited in Scope

In 2002, encouraged by the success of the Vera project, Congress allocated $3 million for alternatives to detention, clarifying that the funds should be used "to promote community-based programs."[340] Over the years, Congress has significantly increased funding for these programs, and by 2009 this funding had increased to $63 million—a $7.2 million enhancement from 2008 as well as $7.2 million above the amount requested by ICE.[341] Nevertheless, the funds are comparatively small, in stark contrast to ICE's $1.7 billion budget allocation for detention bed space. In fact, ICE has budgeted only 2.6 percent of its $2.4 billion detention and removal budget for alternatives to detention programs.[342]

Many—if not most—asylum seekers are not assessed for the possibility of release through an alternatives to detention program. ICE has advised Human Rights First and other groups that it does not track how many of the individuals placed into alternatives to detention programs are asylum seekers.

A number of successful programs have been tested by ICE in recent years, with significant cost savings for the U.S. government. These programs generally allow for release of individual immigration detainees—who are found not to be a threat to the public or a flight risk—from immigration detention, with some additional measures to monitor the individual upon release.[343] The level of supervision generally becomes less restrictive over time. These supervision measures often include regular reporting to an immigration office, home visits, telephone reporting with voice recognition—and requiring the individual to wear an electronic monitoring device (an ankle bracelet). In some cases however, the reporting requirements have been onerous—requiring for example that an asylum seeker report on a weekly basis to a location that is several hours away from their home or restricting the asylum seeker's movements through a very restrictive curfew. These kinds of requirements can pose obstacles to the individual's work and family responsibilities.

A Sri Lankan fisherman, who was a victim of kidnapping by the Liberation Tigers of Tamil Eelam (LTTE), was detained for 30 months in the United States while ICE opposed his request for asylum on the ground that his payment of his ransom consisted "material support" to the armed group. When he was finally released from detention pending a decision by the Board of Immigration Appeals, he was placed into a restrictive supervision program. He was fitted with an ankle bracelet and initially required to report on a monthly basis. Eventually, this was reduced to in-person reporting every six months. After nearly two years of compliance with all reporting requirements, following his 30 months of detention, the fisherman is still required to wear a large ankle bracelet and is subject to home visits.

Currently, there are two ICE supervision and reporting programs in operation: the Intensive Supervision Appearance Program (ISAP) and the Enhanced Supervision/Reporting Program (ESR).

The ISAP was launched in June 2004 and is managed by the private contractor Behavioral Interactions. It was originally piloted in eight cities—Baltimore; Denver; Kansas City, Missouri; Miami; Philadelphia; Portland, Oregon; San Francisco; and St. Paul, Minnesota—and has since been launched in an additional four cities—Delray Beach, Florida; Los Angeles; New York City; and Orlando. Each city has the capacity to enroll approximately 200 individuals. Under ISAP, participants initially wear an ankle bracelet or report in person or by telephone to a case manager.[344] ISAP participants receive a list of free legal and social service providers, as well as information on transportation, translation services, educational institutions, consulate contacts, and homeless shelters.[345] In addition, the case manager works with the individual to identify a "sponsor" or guarantor. The ISAP program initially cost $21 per day, but when the contract with the Behavioral Interactions was renegotiated in 2007, the cost was reduced to $14 a day.[346]

The ESR program was launched in fiscal year 2008 and is also managed by a private contractor—Group 4 Securicor (G4S).[347] Its implementation replaced an earlier program, known as the Electronic Monitoring Program, which was very similar in scope. ESR is available to individuals living within 50 miles of one of the 24 ICE Field Offices and 3 ICE sub-offices.[348] DHS has described ESR as a "more effective monitoring program...providing structured and closely supervised electronic monitoring, residence verification, home visits, in-person reporting and document requirements for program participants."[349] The ESR also provides a separate electronic monitoring program which can be made available to individuals regardless of their location. The ESR program costs an average of $10 a day, and ICE projected 7,000 participants during fiscal year 2009.[350]

Appearance rates for these alternatives to detention programs have shown that they are successful. ICE has reported that individuals participating in the ISAP program had a 99 percent appearance rate for hearings, a 95 percent appearance rate for final removal hearings, and a 91 percent compliance rate with removal orders. The ESR program has a 98 percent appearance rate for hearings, a 93 percent appearance rate for final removal hearings, and a 63 percent compliance rate with removal orders.[351] The ESR program is centered more squarely on forms of electronic monitoring, and does not provide even the limited community-based support—in the form of information and referrals to community and legal services—that ISAP participants receive.

Despite the existence of these programs, the numbers of individuals released into alternative programs is small, especially compared with the number of individuals detained on an annual basis. In March 2009, ICE reported that it had only 17,400 participants in alternatives to detention programs.[352] By contrast, during 2009, ICE expects to detain more than 440,000 individuals.

Alternatives to Detention?

ICE's "alternatives to detention" programs have focused largely on the use of electronic monitoring rather than other supervision models. Both ISAP and ESR provide for electronic monitoring, at least during the initial stages of the program. Though in some cases the level of supervision "ratchets down" and electronic monitoring is eliminated, in many cases electronic monitoring is continued even after the asylum seeker has been regularly complying with program requirements for months.

Such intensive use of electronic monitoring—especially when combined with other restrictive monitoring measures such as curfews, regular check-ins, and home visits—can sometimes essentially constitute a form of "house arrest," or continued detention, rather than a meaningful alternative *to* detention.

In addition, in recent years, ICE appears to have used alternatives to detention to monitor or restrict the movement of asylum seekers and other immigrants who would not otherwise have been detained—in effect using these measures as an "alternative to release."[353] In some cases, ICE has briefly detained asylum seekers who have applied for asylum affirmatively (a population that is not normally detained)—essentially for the purpose of placing them into one of its "alternatives to detention" programs. In other cases, asylum seekers who have been ruled by U.S. immigration courts to be "refugees" who are entitled to withholding of their removal, have been placed into these programs instead of being released from detention without additional supervision. For example:

Ankle bracelet for Guinean torture survivor who applied for asylum affirmatively in Minnesota: A Guinean torture survivor was enrolled in the ISAP program when his case was referred to the immigration court by an asylum officer. He had never been detained previously, and had no criminal record. Initially, he was required to wear an ankle bracelet and report to ISAP in person three times per week, plus be at home one day a week. He received two warnings at work because he had to leave work during his lunch hour for his check-ins and he was sometimes late returning to work. He was embarrassed and ashamed of the ankle bracelet, which he said made him feel like a criminal. Even after the ankle bracelet was removed, he remained on supervision for more than a year. He continues to be required to check in every month, even though he was granted withholding of removal and cannot be returned to Guinea.[354]

Ankle bracelet for Haitian asylum seeker in Florida: In the summer of 2008, a young Haitian woman was taken into custody by ICE officers after she exited the courtroom where she had just submitted her asylum application. She was enrolled into an alternatives to detention program and an ankle bracelet was put onto her leg. She was required to report every two weeks as part of ISAP. Even after she married a legal permanent resident who filed a relative petition for her, she continued to be subject to the check-in requirements and the ankle bracelet.[355]

Ankle bracelet and other supervision for Congolese torture survivor: A Congolese torture survivor, who had not previously been detained, was enrolled in the ISAP program while his asylum case was pending before the immigration court. Though over time his reporting requirements became less onerous, he was initially placed on an ankle bracelet. The ankle bracelet remained on his leg during his appeal to the Board of Immigration Appeals, and after his case was remanded back to the immigration judge. He was finally granted asylum by the immigration court and only then was his ankle bracelet removed.[356]

ICE has confirmed its intent to use alternatives to detention programs to cast a wider net on the population it monitors, stating that it "is expanding the [alternatives to detention] program to encompass a larger portion of the non-detained docket."[357]

Recommendations

The United States should bring its laws and practices relating to immigration detention in line with international standards and U.S. traditions of fairness. The United States has pledged to treat those who seek asylum in accordance with its commitment to the Refugee Convention and Protocol and the International Covenant on Civil and Political Rights, which prohibits arbitrary detention.

Under international standards, asylum seekers should generally not be detained. When they are detained, the detention should have adequate safeguards, including procedures to ensure review by an independent authority or court. Alternatives to detention should be used. And when an asylum seeker is detained, he or she should not be held in penal or prison-like conditions. Detention policies should not discriminate against asylum seekers on the grounds of race, religion, national origin, or any other immutable characteristic.

Thorough reform of the U.S. detention system will require a comination of legislative, regulatory and administrative actions. We have outlined below a series of significant changes that will improve U.S. detention policies and practices in general and for the victims of persecution who seek this country's protection.

1. Review of Detention by the Immigration Courts

The Departments of Justice and Homeland Security should revise current regulatory language to provide arriving asylum seekers with the chance to have their custody reviewed in a hearing before an immigration court, a safeguard afforded other immigration detainees.[358] In revising these provisions, the regulations should make clear that any bond requirements should be appropriate to the circumstances and means of the asylum seeker, and that the immigration courts can direct that an individual be released into an alternatives to detention program.

The U.S. Congress should enact legislation providing these asylum seekers with access to immigration court custody hearings to ensure lasting change by putting this change into law as well.

2. Other Reforms to Limit Unnecessary Detention

In addition to ensuring immigration court review of detention for asylum seekers, the **Department of Homeland Security** and **Immigration and Customs Enforcement** should reform the parole process and create a nationwide program for supervised release or other alternatives to detention.

■ **Reform the Parole Process**.

• **Regulations based on prior criteria**: The Department of Homeland Security, Immigration and Customs Enforcement, should issue regulations providing for the release of an asylum seeker who can establish identity, has ties to the community, satisfies the credible fear standard, and does not pose a danger to the community. These regulations should require that *all* arriving asylum seekers be assessed for parole eligibility after passing through the credible fear process.

• **Stop detaining those found to be refugees**: ICE should stop its local practice of detaining individuals who have been granted withholding of removal or protection under the Convention Against Torture. ICE should stop using the regulation that allows for a period to arrange for possible deportation to a third country as a justification for extending by 90 days the detention of these individuals. The new parole regulations, or any new parole policy, should provide for the release of individuals determined by the immigration court to be entitled to asylum or withholding of removal and who do not present a risk to the community—as did the February 9, 2004, ICE guidance.

■ **Create a Nationwide System of Supervised Release.** When an asylum seeker is not eligible for release on parole and some additional supervision is determined to be necessary, the individual should be assessed for release to a supervised release program or other alternative to detention. The **Department of Homeland Security, Immigration and Customs Enforcement,** should significantly expand the existing framework and create a nationwide system using community-based alternatives to detention programs. These programs should be administered in partnership with community-based organizations and should be full service programs, incorporating case managers, referrals to legal and social service providers and assistance with accessing information about court and case information. These programs should be used to secure the release from detention of individuals who are not otherwise eligible for parole but who present no risk to the community.

- **Individualized assessment:** The level and kind of supervision should be determined after an individualized determination, rather than through a system that automatically places ankle bracelets on all individuals. The individual should be able to seek review of this determination through an immigration court custody hearing.

- **Ankle bracelets:** Electronic monitoring devices (ankle bracelets) should only be used when determined to be necessary, and they should not be used in a manner that restricts freedom of movement to such an extent as to essentially constitute continued custody.

Congress should:

■ **Enact** legislation mandating the regulations and other measures necessary to reform the parole process for asylum seekers (which are outlined above), if the Department of Homeland Security does not implement those reforms, and requiring DHS to implement a nationwide program of alternatives to detention, contracting with community-based organizations (as described above).

■ **Appropriate** funding for alternatives to detention and redirect the savings realized from detention to alternatives to detention, leading to an overall cost savings.

3. Stop Using Jail-like Facilities

The Department of Homeland Security and **Immigration and Customs Enforcement** should stop using jails and jail-like facilities to detain asylum seekers and other immigration detainees. The Department should also end the practice of detaining families. Instead, asylum seekers should be:

■ Released from detention on parole or through an immigration court custody hearing if they meet the applicable criteria; or

■ Released to a supervised release program, or other alternative to detention program, if some supervision of the release is necessary.

When asylum seekers are detained—during the period of initial "mandatory" detention under the U.S. expedited removal statute, or if continued detention is determined to be necessary after a fair and individualized assessment—they should not be held in penal or prison-like facilities, but rather in facilities where the they can wear their own clothing and the conditions of their detention are not prison-like, as outlined below.

The Department of Homeland Security and **Immigration and Customs Enforcement** should immediately review all facilities, identify and implement changes that can be made promptly (such as changes in uniforms, handcuffing policies, and movement within the facility), and identify which facilities should no longer be used.

Congress should also prohibit the detention of asylum seekers in prison-like conditions and should require DHS to provide an assessment of changes that it will make to end the detention of asylum seekers in penal conditions.

4. Stop Opening Remote Facilities and Ensure Adequate Legal and Other Support *Prior* to Using Facilities

The Department of Homeland Security should direct and **Immigration and Customs Enforcement** should take steps to:

■ Stop opening and using facilities located in remote areas that are far from legal representation resources, immigration courts, or an adequate pool of medical staff.

■ Ensure that legal orientation presentations, adequate legal representation, full medical staffing, immigration judges and asylum officers in person (and not by video conferencing), and pastoral care are actually in place and funded *before* detaining asylum seekers or other immigrants at a facility—working with the Department of Justice and U.S. Citizenship and Immigration Services as well as legal, religious, community, and other nongovernmental stakeholders.

■ Ensure that Immigration and Customs Enforcement officers are in regular communication with asylum seeker and immigrant detainees, including those held at county and local jails. Steps should include increasing the presence of officers at facilities and implementing an effective method for detainees to speak to Immigration and Customs Enforcement officers—other than leaving messages that are not returned.

The Department of Justice should:

■ **Implement Nationwide Legal Orientation Presentations:** The Department of Justice should seek appropriate funding to expand legal orientation programs to *all* detention facilities and jails used to hold asylum seekers and other immigration detainees. While not a substitute for legal counsel, these presentations promote fundamental fairness and improve the efficiency of the courts.

■ **End the Use of Video Asylum Hearings:** The Department of Justice should direct the immigration courts to stop conducting asylum hearings by video conferencing, and should request and allocate funding to ensure that the immigration courts can conduct in-person hearings at detention centers.

Congress should:

■ **Appropriate** funds to expand Legal Orientation Programs nationwide so that all asylum seekers and others in immigration detention receive access to legal information and assistance in assessing their legal options.

■ **Ensure** adequate funding to both the immigration courts and the asylum office so that they can conduct asylum hearings and screening interviews in person rather than by video.

5. Improve the Conditions of Detention

■ **Detention Should not be Based on a Penal Model**
The detention standards used by the Department of Homeland Security for the detention of asylum seekers should be revised to provide for detention in which individuals can, for example: wear their own clothing (rather than prison uniforms); have contact visitation (as opposed to visits through plexi-glass barriers) with family and friends; and have freedom of movement within the secure facility (so they can use outdoor areas, libraries, indoor recreation, or cafeteria areas during the course of the day). Officers should not wear prison guard uniforms, but should be dressed in an alternate uniform, such as a white shirt and tan pants. Handcuffs and shackles should not be used (in general and during transportation) absent extraordinary circumstances. Some of these changes could, and should, be made at some facilities immediately.

■ **Medical and Mental Health Care Must Be Improved**
The Department of Homeland Security and ICE should take steps to improve the provision of medical and mental health care at all facilities where asylum seekers and other immigrant detainees are held, seeking input from independent experts and medical professionals, many of whom have provided detailed recommendations on improving medical care.[359] These reforms should include steps to ensure that:

• Medical units have an appropriate level of staffing *prior* to detaining asylum seekers and other immigrants at a facility, and a mechanism is in place to ensure that detainees are removed from facilities that do not have adequate medical staffing.

• Interpretation services are appropriately used during medical visits at all facilities, including by creating a mechanism and/or form to evaluate

and monitor the use of interpreters by medical staff at facilities.

• Mental health care should include specialized counseling for survivors of torture and trauma.

Congress should continue to provide increased oversight to issues relating to detainee health care and deaths, and should pass legislation mandating improved medical care and the independent investigation of detainee deaths.

6. Protection Mechanisms at the Department of Homeland Security

The Secretary of Homeland Security should:

■ **Create an Asylum and Refugee Protection Office Within the DHS Secretary's Office.** This office should ensure that policies, practices and legal interpretations relating to asylum seekers and refugees are consistent with this country's legal commitments and that the reforms recommended in this report are implemented. This office should be provided with the resources, staffing and authority to oversee policies and practices relating to asylum seekers and refugees throughout the Department of Homeland Security. The office should have both operational and policy oversight of the various immigration agencies on asylum and refugee issues, and should be headed by a political appointee, with extensive experience in refugee issues, who reports directly to the Department of Homeland Security Secretary. This senior official should have at least eight staff members who are responsible for areas that include: legal standards for detention and parole, parole and release policies and practices; detention conditions, including medical and mental health care and legal access; inspections and expedited removal; border patrol and expedited removal; Coast Guard, interdiction and asylum/migration issues; refugee resettlement issues; and the U.S. asylum adjudication system.

■ **Maintain a Senior Refugee and Asylum Policy Position.** The Secretary should maintain a Senior Refugee and Asylum Policy position in the DHS policy office, and provide that position with sufficient staffing and resources. This position should report directly to the DHS Assistant Secretary for Policy.

■ **Strengthen the Deputy Secretary's Capacity** and chain-of-command authority, in order to increase coordination across bureaus on refugee and asylum matters, and to ensure that the Asylum and Refugee Protection Office's directives and guidance are followed by the various immigration-related agencies.

■ **Direct the DHS General Counsel to Make Asylum Seeker and Refugee Protection a Priority** by ensuring compliance, throughout the Department of Homeland Security, with refugee and human rights treaty obligations. The new Department of Homeland Security General Counsel should set up mechanisms to ensure that Coast Guard, Immigration and Customs Enforcement, Customs and Border Protection and U.S. Citizenship and Immigration Services policies and actions are in accordance with U.S. treaty obligations. To ensure that positions and actions of Department of Homeland Security "trial attorneys" are in accord with U.S. treaty obligations, these attorneys should be redeployed from Immigration and Customs Enforcement to a new litigation unit within the General Counsel's office. The General Counsel should also create the position of Associate General Counsel for Refugee and Asylum Matters.

7. Provide Timely and Accurate Statistics

The **Department of Homeland Security** should ensure that **Immigration and Customs Enforcement** improves its systems for tracking data relating to the detention of asylum seekers, including data reflecting the number of detained asylum seekers, their age, their gender, the location of their detention, the length of their detention, and their parole or release from detention. This informa-tion, which is required by law to be provided annually to Congress and to the public on request (under 8 U.S.C. §§ 1377-1378), should be provided to both Congress and the public immediately after the end of each fiscal year in a timely manner.

8. Improve Conduct of Expedited Removal

The **Department of Homeland Security** should ensure that **Customs and Border Protection** implements critical reforms recommended by the U.S. Commission on International Religious Freedom and ensures that procedures designed to protect asylum seekers from being returned to their persecution are followed. In particular, the Department of Homeland Security and Customs and Border Protection should:

■ Stop detaining asylum seekers who arrive with valid visas that are considered invalid by Customs and Border Protection solely because the individual requests asylum or indicates a fear of return.

■ Ensure Customs and Border Protection officers ask all required questions aimed at ensuring that a refugee is not mistakenly deported, and ensure that any officer who fails to do so is disciplined and no longer permitted to perform this function.

U.S. Citizenship and Immigration Services should direct and the Asylum Division should take steps to:

■ Ensure that *all* credible fear interviews are conducted in a timely manner and request and allocate appropriate funding so that such interviews are conducted in person. If Immigration and Customs Enforcement stops locating detention facilities in remote areas, the reasons for using video conferencing for credible fear interviews should decrease significantly.

■ Conduct an assessment of the decline in the credible fear grant rate, the decline in referrals for credible fear interviews and the impact of video conferencing on the conduct and outcomes of credible fear interviews.

Congress should authorize the U.S. Commission on International Religious Freedom to conduct a review of the expanded use of expedited removal and its impact on asylum seekers, and should appropriate funding for this assessment.

Appendix

Methodology

Human Rights First has monitored DHS and ICE detention policies and practices relating to asylum seekers since the Department of Homeland Security took over responsibility for asylum and immigration matters. Through our legal representation program, which provides pro bono representation to refugees seeking asylum in the U.S. and legal orientation presentations to detained asylum seekers and other immigrants, we have interviewed hundreds of detained asylum seekers and other immigrant detainees. During 2008 and 2009, Human Rights First conducted additional research relating to the U.S. detention of asylum seekers. This research included:

- Visits to and tours of more than ten detention facilities—the South Texas Detention Center and the Willacy Detention Center in Texas; the Elizabeth Detention Center in New Jersey; the Columbia Care Center facility in South Carolina; the Regional Correctional Center in New Mexico; the El Paso Processing Center in Texas; and the Hampton Roads Regional Jail and the Piedmont county jail in Virginia. Other facilities visited by Human Rights staff in the course of our *pro bono* legal work and detention monitoring include the Hudson county jail, Monmouth county jail, and Sussex county jail in New Jersey. Human Rights First also sought access to additional facilities in California and Illinois, but was denied access by ICE, which cited pending litigation at those facilities.

- Meetings and follow-up correspondence with national immigration officials, including officials from ICE and DHS more broadly, as well as with local ICE officials and contract staff including during tours of the facilities;

- Interviews with nearly 30 formerly detained refugees and asylum seekers who were detained in U.S. immigration facilities before being granted asylum, in addition to the many others we have interviewed through the course of our work. This included Human Rights First clients as well as individuals assisted by *pro bono* organizations in other areas of the country. These refugees were detained at over a dozen different facilities, including the Elizabeth Detention Center, the Otay Detention Facility, the El Paso Processing Center, the McHenry County Jail, the Port Isabel Processing Center, and the Hampton Roads Regional Jail.

- Interviews with more than 15 detained refugees, asylum seekers, and other immigrants during our visits of detention facilities.

- Interviews and correspondence with more than 30 faith-based and other *pro bono* legal service providers as well as social service and religious support providers. Human Rights First staff interviewed individuals from around the country, including organizations operating in Arizona, California, Colorado, Florida, Illinois, Louisiana, Massachusetts, Minnesota, New Jersey, New Mexico, New York, Texas, Virginia, Washington, and Wisconsin.

- Seeking statistics and other information from the Executive Office of Immigration Review, Department of Justice, and ICE, including through a series of Freedom of Information Act requests.

- Reviewing government reports—including reports by the DHS Office of Inspector General and the Government Accountability Office.

Abbreviations and Glossary of Terms

CBP	U.S. Customs and Border Protection
CCA	Corrections Corporation of America
DHS	Department of Homeland Security
DOJ	Department of Justice
EOIR	Executive Office for Immigration Review
ESR	Enhanced Supervision/Reporting
FOIA	Freedom of Information Act
ICE	U.S. Immigration and Customs Enforcement
INA	U.S. Immigration and Nationality Act
ISAP	Intensive Supervision Appearance Program
LOP	Legal Orientation Program
UNHCR	United Nations High Commissioner for Refugees
USCIRF	U.S. Commission on International Religious Freedom
USCIS	U.S. Citizenship and Immigration Services

Arriving asylum seeker—An asylum seeker who arrives at a port of entry, such as an airport or border crossing, and expresses a fear of returning to his or her country of origin. Arriving asylum seekers are considered "arriving aliens," and, under 8 CFR §1003.19(h)(2)(i)(B), are precluded by regulation from receiving custody determination hearings in front of an immigration judge. Arriving asylum seekers are subject to mandatory detention until they pass the "credible fear" screening interview.

Credible fear interview—An interview conducted by a USCIS asylum officer to determine if the asylum applicant has a credible fear of persecution—defined under the law as a significant possibility of being granted asylum—from his or her country of origin. If the applicant passes the credible fear interview, he or she is put into removal proceedings and can then apply for asylum in front of an immigration judge.

Custody determination hearing—Certain aliens are eligible for a hearing in front of an immigration judge to review ICE's custody determination. The immigration judge may order the release of an individual on bond or on his or her own recognizance. Arriving asylum seekers are not given this opportunity to have a custody decision reviewed by an immigration judge under certain regulatory provisions.

Expedited removal—The process of expedited removal gives U.S. immigration inspectors and border patrol officers—instead of immigration judges—the power to order people deported. It applies to people who arrive without travel documents or with false documents at airports and borders, as well as to those apprehended within 100 miles of the border and 14 days of their entry. Those who express a fear of return are supposed to be referred for "credible fear" screening interviews. They are also subject to "mandatory detention."

ICE Detention Standards—Guidelines issued by ICE that specify conditions for facilities, treatment, and health care in detention centers. The standards have not been codified as regulations, and are therefore not legally enforceable. A new set of "performance based" standards—also non-binding—was released in 2008 and will be fully implemented in 2010.

Legal Orientation Program (LOP)—The Executive Office of Immigration Review in the Department of Justice, contracts with nonprofit organizations to carry out Legal Orientation Programs at a limited number of detention locations throughout the country. The LOP consists of group presentations, individual orientation sessions, self-help legal resources, and assistance in obtaining pro bono representation.

Profiles of Detention Facilities

The South Texas (Pearsall) Detention Center, Pearsall, Texas

The South Texas Detention Center, more commonly known simply as the Pearsall detention center, is located in Pearsall, Texas, about an hour south of San Antonio. The 2,300 square foot facility was built in 2005 to hold 1,020 immigration detainees, but it was quickly expanded to its current capacity of 1,904 beds in response to the launching of the Secure Border Initiative, a DHS policy that calls for expanded expedited removal and increased detention.[360] Human Rights First visited the facility in May 2008, accompanied by *pro bono* attorneys and representatives of local faith and community groups, and met with officials at the facility.

The Facility

Though the GEO Group—the private contractor that contracts with ICE to manage the facility—refers to the Pearsall facility as a "minimum security"[361] facility, the detention center is a prison in just about every sense of the word. Asylum seekers and other immigrant detainees arrive at the Pearsall detention center handcuffed. The detainees are stripped of their personal property and receive prison uniforms. Detainees are held in "pods," some holding as many as 100 detainees, in which they eat, sleep, and use the showers and toilets separated from the rest of the room only by a low wall. They sleep on narrow bunk beds, with two or three sets of bunk beds lined up head-to-toe. An officer is present in each pod throughout the day. Each pod is connected to what the facility considers to be an "outdoor recreation" area—a courtyard surrounded by high walls with a mesh ceiling. Though not truly "outdoor," detainees do have fairly steady access to this area during the day. All detainees are counted several times a day, in a process that often lasts an hour and requires that all detainees stand by their beds.

The Pearsall detention center has 36 individual cells that it uses for administrative and disciplinary segregation. Detainees in segregation are kept in the same small room throughout the day and have a similar recreation area which they can access one at a time. There are also two additional units in the segregation area for detainees with a history of violent crimes, which together hold 130 detainees.

Though the ICE detention standards state that the visiting area "shall be appropriately furnished and arranged, and as comfortable and pleasant as practicable,"[362] detainees who receive visits by family members or friends, can only see and speak to the visitors through a plexiglass partition. Furthermore, family and friends may only visit during designated hours on Saturdays and Sundays.

The facility holds a range of immigration detainees and asylum seekers—many without criminal records.

Asylum Seekers

During the 2007 fiscal year, more than 2,700 asylum seekers were held at the detention center, and in September, 2008 alone, 200 asylum seekers subject to the expedited removal process were detained at the facility. According to an estimate by ICE, asylum seekers who go through the credible fear process are detained an average of 75 days, though of course they acknowledged that some detainees are detained much longer as their cases wind their way through the appeals process. Local legal service providers reported having asylum clients from all over the world, including Burma, El Salvador, Eritrea, Ethiopia, Honduras, and Somalia.

At the time ICE provided its responses in September 2008, there were 47 asylum seekers who had been detained for more than three months, 23 who had been detained for over six months, and 14 who had been detained for a year or longer.

Access to Justice and Legal Representation

The Pearsall detention center is located in a remote and sparsely populated area about an hour south of San Antonio, and two hours south of Austin, where most pro bono representation organizations are located. This clearly limits the legal representation that is available to detained asylum seekers and other immigrants, as it is difficult for under-resourced nonprofit organizations to travel to the detention center for client meetings.

Though the facility can hold over 1,900 detainees, it has only three attorney visitation rooms. Local ICE officials stated that three visitation rooms were deemed sufficient for the original building plan of just over 1,000 detainees, and that there had been no consideration of increasing the number of legal visitation rooms when the facility was expanded. The facility appears to be modeled on a criminal facility, and not tailored for immigrant detainees who are in the midst of their immigration court proceedings. As a result, attorneys report regularly having to wait long periods of time—sometimes several hours—in order to speak with their clients. Pro bono representatives in the area find themselves limited in how many detained cases they can take on for representation simply because they cannot travel the distance to Pearsall and meet with clients.

An Austin-based organization—American Gateways (formerly the Political Asylum Project of Austin, PAPA)—provides Legal Orientation Presentations to immigrant detainees at the Pearsall detention center. Though the facility opened in June 2005, the presentations did not begin until October 2006, well over a year after the facility began detaining asylum seekers and other immigrants. Now, presentations are given three times a week to detainees in removal proceedings before their first hearing in immigration court.

According to local ICE officials, only asylum seekers who make an affirmative request for parole are considered for release. In practice, this means that unrepresented asylum seekers—who probably will only have limited information regarding the process and face difficulties in gaining access to the documents necessary to make a successful parole request—are unlikely to be released on paroled. When asked about the eligibility criteria for parole, the ICE Assistant Field Office Director at the facility listed establishing identity, not being a flight risk, and serving the public interest as the criteria considered in making a decision. A representative from a local pro bono organization representing asylum seekers at the facility reported that all parole requests she had made in 2008 had been denied. Asylum seekers who requested protection at U.S. border entry points are not allowed to have the immigration court review the need for their continued detention—rather they may only be released through the parole process. Other immigration detainees are allowed to have these immigration court hearings.

Credible fear interviews—screening interviews that will determine whether they can apply for asylum or be summarily deported—for asylum seekers at the facility are conducted by video conferencing, and sometimes even by telephone. In addition, all court hearings—including the final hearing at which an asylum seeker testifies—are held by video conferencing, with the detainee sitting in an empty courtroom inside the detention center while the judge appears on a television screen. A recent study demonstrated that asylum seekers who have their immigration court asylum hearings conducted by video are about half as likely to be granted asylum.[363]

The Willacy Detention Center, Raymondville, Texas

The Willacy Detention Center—nicknamed "Tent City" and "Ritmo"—is the largest immigration jail in the country. It sits in the southernmost part of Texas. Originally built in 2006 to hold 2,000 detainees, it expanded in the summer of 2008 to a capacity of 3,000. The facility is operated by the Management & Training Corporation (MTC), a for-profit contractor that also manages another large immigration detention center located in New Mexico. Human Rights First toured the facility, accompanied by *pro bono* attorneys and representatives of local faith and community groups, and spoke with local ICE officials in May 2008.

The Facility

The detention center consists of ten large tents made of heavy white fabric stretched over metal beams, each holding 200 detainees, and a separate cement building with 1,000 additional beds. The outdoor paths leading to the tents and to the brick building are dotted with guard posts. The tents are divided into four large dormitories—or "pods"—each with 50 beds. Both the male and female pods are similar in set-up, and detainees eat, sleep, and use the toilet in the same large area. Detainees sleep on narrow metal bunk beds, and the bathroom area is located behind a short wall, offering little privacy. There are no divisions between individual toilets and showers, giving detainees no privacy while using the facilities. The expansion building—a cement building—consists of 20 pods, each with 50 beds. Again, the bathroom area is located behind only a short wall, with sinks located directly above the toilets. The new building also contains 43 segregation cells.

When detainees are first brought to the facility, they are placed in large holding cells of 25 to 50 people. They are then brought to the "intake" area, where they are fingerprinted, photographed, and given prison-like color coded uniforms in blue, orange, or red. Detainees then undergo the initial medical screening, provided within 12 hours of arrival at the facility. At the time of Human Rights First's visit, Division of Immigration Health Services (DIHS) officials stated they had a number of vacancies in the medical department, including eight vacancies for registered nurses. The detention center had only one physician and a psychiatrist who was available only two days a week. ICE declined to answer follow-up questions on the number of vacancies, including medical vacancies, at the facility in the fall of 2008. In May 2008, around the same time as Human Rights First's visit, the Washington Post also reported that the facility had no clinical director or pharmacist.[364]

At the time of Human Rights First's visit, the law library was held in a small trailer. Detainees have access to the library on weekdays for two and a half hours, with male detainees scheduled in the morning and female detainees scheduled for the afternoon. The small library contained a limited selection of U.S. laws—including some outdated materials—and two computers.

Asylum Seekers

In May 2008, there were just over 1,700 detainees at the facility (which then had a capacity of 2,000). According to data provided by local ICE officials, approximately 550 asylum seekers were detained at the facility during fiscal year 2007. This included individuals from Burma, Colombia, Eritrea, Haiti, Liberia, Pakistan, Somalia, and Uganda.

Asylum seekers who are apprehended along the border may be transported to a number of detention facilities in southern Texas, including Willacy. Detainees at the Willacy facility who express a fear of return to their country are referred for credible fear interviews and transferred to the South Texas Detention Center in Pearsall, over four hours away. This is generally the case even for detainees who have been able to obtain local representation while at the Willacy facility.

The majority of detainees at Willacy at the time of Human Rights First's visit to the facility had been placed in the expedited removal process, and therefore did not have proceedings pending before an immigration court. Many are being "processed" for deportation. ICE officials stated that the average stay at the facility was only 18 days for this population. ICE officials also stated there were a "handful" of individuals who had been ordered removed and had spent more than 180 days in detention awaiting their removal. In addition, according to local pro bono legal service providers, some asylum seekers are transferred to Willacy from other facilities after passing their credible fear interviews.

Access to Legal Representation

There are only a handful of *pro bono* legal organizations in the area. ProBAR—a program staffed by only two attorneys that works with pro bono attorneys to provide representation to asylum seekers—is the only organization that represents asylum seekers on a pro bono basis, but is also one of the few pro bono organizations that represents detainees at the nearby 1,200-bed Port Isabel facility.

Though the detention center opened in 2006, Legal Orientation Presentations did not begin at Willacy until November 2008, more than two years later. These presentations are conducted by Texas RioGrande Legal Aid (TRLA), however, due to funding restrictions, TRLA cannot provide representation to undocumented individuals, including arriving asylum seekers.

Elizabeth Detention Center, Elizabeth, New Jersey

A former warehouse in an industrial district of Elizabeth, New Jersey, now serves as a 300-bed immigration detention center. The facility first opened in the early 1990s under the management of Esmor Correctional Services, but has been operated by the Corrections Corporation of America—a private contractor that manages a number of other immigration detention facilities across the country—since 1997.

The Facility

The detention center—a former warehouse—holds up to 300 individuals, both men and women. It is operated by Corrections Corporation of America (CCA), the largest private for-profit company that operates a number of other immigration detention facilities throughout the country, including in Texas and California.

The detention center holds only non-criminal detainees that are classified as low security. However, when asylum seekers are detained at nearby airports, they are transported to the detention facility in handcuffs and shackles. Upon arrival, detainees are stripped of their clothing and property, and issued navy blue uniforms and identity bracelets. They are then assigned a bed and accompanying "bed number." The guards use these numbers to refer to the detainees instead of using their names. Asylum seekers and other detainees are held in large pod areas, where a short wall partitions the sleeping and eating area from the toilets and showers.

Detainees are counted several times a day, including early in the morning, after lunch, in the afternoon, after dinner, and one or more times during the night. The only "outdoor" recreation area available is a courtyard surrounded by high walls with a metal grate as a ceiling. Detainees interviewed by Human Rights First staff reported having the opportunity to access this area daily on weekdays, but also reported that they must sometimes choose between recreation and having time to access the law library.

As in many other facilities, asylum seekers and other immigrants detained at the Elizabeth facility do not have access to contact visits with friends and family members. Instead, if they receive visitors they can only speak with them through a plexi-glass separator, using a telephone. Three small attorney visitation rooms are available for visits with legal representatives.

Slightly more than a third of individuals detained at the Elizabeth Detention Center are in immigration court proceedings. The rest have received an order of removal and are either appealing their cases in federal court, trying to reopen their cases, or awaiting deportation. As of early February 2009, there were 22 individuals who had been detained at Elizabeth for more than six months.

Asylum Seekers

Arriving asylum seekers who are apprehended at the Newark Liberty International Airport in New Jersey or the John F. Kennedy International Airport in New York and placed into expedited removal proceedings are often brought to the Elizabeth Detention Center. In recent years, these asylum seekers have come from a range of places including Eritrea, Guinea, Haiti, Ivory Coast, Liberia, Somalia, Tibet, Togo, and Zimbabwe. Asylum seekers found to have a credible fear of persecution are then referred for immigration court proceedings. Human Rights First has provided representation to dozens of asylum seekers at the detention center over the past several years. Asylum seekers who are not paroled prior to being granted asylum by the immigration court often spend four months or longer in detention. Those who pursue appeals can spend many more months or even years detained.

A February 2005 U.S. Commission on International Religious Freedom study reported the parole rate for asylum seekers at the facility was 3.8 percent.[365] In recent months, Human Rights First has noted an increase in the parole rate at this facility. This shift may be partly the result of the new policy, or a consequence of new local ICE leadership with oversight of the New Jersey facility, or both. From October 2008 through January 2009, for example, thirteen asylum seekers submitted parole requests. Of these, 10—or 77 percent—were granted.

Access to Legal Representation

Legal orientation presentations are conducted regularly for newly arrived detainees at the facility by four local nonprofit organizations, including Human Rights First. The organizations receive a list of newly arrived detainees from ICE, and then provide all detainees who attend the presentations with information on the immigration and detention systems. They also take steps to assist detainees to secure pro bono representation, but given limited resources and the lack of government funding for representation, some immigration detainees do not secure representation. Despite these efforts, some detained asylum seekers do not receive pro bono representation and cannot afford private representation, and so are left to navigate their case unrepresented.

Varick Street Federal Detention Facility, New York, New York

The Varick Street Federal Detention Facility is located on the fourth floor of a federal building in downtown Manhattan. The facility was previously operated as a detention center until it closed its doors soon after 9/11. It reopened as an immigration detention center in February 2008. It is operated under Contract with the Ahtna Technical Services Inc., a for-profit corporation. Human Rights First toured the facility in November 2008.

The Facility

The detention center can hold up to 250 male detainees, and ICE advised us that the population fluctuates between 200 and 250. The detainees are separated into four "pods" each holding 50 to 65 men. The bathroom area—with six showers and several toilets—is separated from the sleeping area, affording at least some privacy. A guard is present in the pods 24 hours a day, and detainees are counted four times a day. Detainees who wish to make phone calls must purchase a calling card from the commissary.

The Varick Street facility does not have an outdoor recreation area. Rather it only has an indoor gym with windows that do not open. As a result, ICE officials at the facility informed Human Rights First staff that detainees may not remain at Varick for long periods of time and are usually transferred to another facility—where "outdoor" recreation is available—after approximately 30 days. However, Human Rights First has been in contact with several detainees who have spent months at the Varick Street facility.

The facility has a small law library with six computers that have legal research software. Detainees may have access to the law library for one hour each day Monday through Friday, and must sign up in advance.

Some religious services are provided at the facility—Catholic services are performed once a week, and an Imam visits the facility from time to time. However, ICE officials noted that there were not many volunteers at the facility, and that they did not have sufficient donations to be able to provide Bibles, Qurans, or other religious texts for free to detainees.

The building also houses its own immigration court with two judges who hear the cases of the individuals detained at the facility. The judges also preside by video conferencing over the cases of immigration detainees who are transferred to one of the county jails in New Jersey.

Asylum Seekers

The facility holds both criminal and non-criminal detainees. If arriving asylum seekers are referred for credible fear interviews they are transferred to the Elizabeth Detention Center in New Jersey. Some other asylum seekers are, however, detained at the facility, sometimes for several months. Since it has reopened, Human Rights First has responded to numerous calls from asylum seekers detained at the facility.

Access to Legal Representation

The location of the Varick Street detention center in Manhattan means that individuals detained at the facility have a wider range of potential legal representation resources available to them. However, asylum seekers and other detainees are not usually detained at the facility for the duration of their cases. They are generally transferred to one of a number of county jails in New Jersey.

The Legal Aid Society of New York began a "Know Your Rights" program (independent of the EOIR's Legal Orientation Program) at the facility in the fall of 2008. Through this program, law students or volunteer attorneys from local law firms visit detainees at the facility on a regular basis to provide them with general information and screen cases for possible representation. In addition, detainees have access to "detention hotlines" through both Legal Aid and Human Rights First.

Response from Immigration and Customs Enforcement

Office of the Assistant Secretary

U.S. Department of Homeland Security
500 12ᵗʰ Street. SW
Washington. DC 20536

**U.S. Immigration
and Customs
Enforcement**

April 28, 2009

Annie Sovcik, Esq.
Advocacy Counsel
Human Rights First
100 Maryland Avenue, NE
Suite 500
Washington, DC 20002-5625

Dear Ms. Sovcik:

Thank you for providing U.S. Immigration and Customs Enforcement with the opportunity to comment on the Human Rights First upcoming report, "U.S. Detention of Asylum Seekers." We value your contributions to the promotion of international human rights, especially for those seeking asylum in the United States, and welcome this opportunity work together.

Secretary Napolitano created the position of Special Advisor at ICE within days of taking office to focus on the significant growth in immigration detention over the last five years and asked me to serve in this capacity. I am dedicating these first months to the close examination of issues impacting detention and removal including arrest priorities, detention decisions and practices, and the utilization of alternatives to detention. I am fortunate to have many resources to inform this early assessment. There are excellent reports by governmental agencies and non-governmental organizations including Human Rights First that I have read. There are exceptional individuals affiliated with these agencies and organizations with whom have spoken, all of them generous with their time and good counsel. There are all types of detention facilities that I have toured and willing detainees in every place with whom I have spoken. There are field data and audits and evaluations of activities in the field that I have reviewed. Shortly, I will present my preliminary findings and first recommendations to Secretary Napolitano. It is my intent that this briefing provides strategies to improve current practices and serve as the basis for measurable and sustainable reform. This will best be done in partnership with others in government and the community.

Your report about the detention of asylum seekers speaks to issues impacting many detainees in ICE custody and contributes to the body of work upon which we can build. It also identifies areas for improvement that we can address immediately. When public documents are requested, they will be provided timely and when those documents are in draft form, they will be forwarded as quickly as they become public records. To that point, I am sending you a copy of the 2007 ICE Parole Policy pursuant to Section 903 of the Haitian Refugee Immigration and Fairness Act today, and will transmit a copy of the 2008 report upon its completion. Likewise, providing Human Rights First with access to detention facilities to conduct its work also enables ICE to better perform its governmental functions. We regret the difficulty you recently encountered at two facilities and are resolved that it should not happen again.

www.ice.gov

Annie Sovcik, Esq
Page 2

I look forward to continuing this conversation and will take the liberty of contacting you to
schedule a meeting.

Sincerely,

Dora Schriro
Special Advisor to the Secretary

Endnotes

[1] Throughout the report, quotes from asylum seekers and refugees are drawn from our interviews of detained and formerly detained asylum seekers, unless otherwise noted. As the majority of these individuals have already been granted asylum by U.S. authorities and have such been recognized as "refugees" by the U.S. government, we will sometimes use the term "refugee" to refer to them.

[2] The total number of asylum seekers was obtained by adding the number of detained asylum seekers for the last 7 months of fiscal year 2003 through February 2009. For years 2003, 2004, and 2006, the number of detained asylum seekers was obtained from ICE's section 903 reports under the Haitian Refugee and Immigration Fairness Act.(ICE, *Report to Congress: Detained Asylum Seekers Fiscal Year 2007 (2008); ICE, Report to Congress Detained Asylum Seekers Fiscal Year 2006* (2007); ICE, *Report to Congress: Detained Asylum Seekers Fiscal Year 2004* (2005); ICE, *Report to Congress: Detained Asylum Seekers Fiscal Year 2003* (2004)). They are 8,137, 11,909, 5,761, and 9,971 respectively. For 2005, 2008, and 2009 (through February), the number of detained asylum seekers was calculated by using the number of individuals who were found to have credible fear of persecution: 8,469 for fiscal year 2005, 3,128 for fiscal year 2008, and 1,618 for the first five months of fiscal year 2009 (credible fear statistics provided by U.S. Citizenship and Immigration Services). No data on the number of affirmative and defensive asylum seekers for these years has been made available by ICE. For each year, the number of asylum seekers was then multiplied by the average length of detention, and then by the average daily cost of detention. The average length of 64 days is used for 2003 as provided in the 2003 report (ICE, *Report to Congress: Detained Asylum Seekers Fiscal Year 2003 (2004))*, and the average length of 71.5 days is used for remaining years, as was reported in the 2004 report – the last year for which this information is provided (ICE, *Report to Congress: Detained Asylum Seekers Fiscal Year 2003* (2004)). The average costs of detention used are $85 for 2003, $80 for 2004, $85 for 2005, $95 for 2006 and 2007, $97 for 2008, and $95 for 2009.

[3] In 2002, the former INS used 20,662 jail-like detention beds (21,262 beds minus 600 beds at the non-jail-like Broward Transitional Center facility). Department of Justice, "Fiscal Year 2000 Performance Report and Fiscal Year 2002 Performance Plan: Strategic Goal Five." This number grew to 33,400 immigration detention beds in 2009. James T. Hayes, Jr., Director, Office of Detention and Removal Operations, "Health Services for Detainees in U.S. Immigrations and Customs Enforcement Custody," before the House Appropriations Committee, Subcommittee on Homeland Security (March 3, 2009).

[4] Jaya Ramji Nogales, Andrew Schoenholtz and Phillip Schrag, *Refugee Roulette: Disparities in asylum adjudication*, 60 Stan. L. Rev. 295, 340 (2007).

[5] 2,723 out of 4,420 credible fear interviews conducted by video in 2007 – all from the Houston asylum office. Information provided by USCIS, at Asylum Office Headquarters liaison meeting (June 17, 2008 and March 9, 2009). Frank M. Walsh and Edward M. Walsh, *Effective Processing or Assembly-Line Justice? The Use of Teleconferencing in Asylum Removal Hearings*, 22 Geo. Immigr. L.J. 259, 271 (2008).

[6] The regulations on parole state that aliens may only be paroled if "the aliens present neither a security risk nor a risk of absconding." 8 C.F.R. § 212.5. The most recent ICE guidelines on parole, as well as the previous guidance from 1997 and 1998, also provide that parole may only be considered for those who are not a flight or security risk. ICE, "Parole of Arriving Aliens Found to Have a 'Credible Fear'" (Nov 6, 2007). Also, see, e.g., *Matter of Patel*, 15 I.&N. Dec. 666 (BIA 1976); *Matter of Spiliopoulos*, 16 I&N Dec.488 (BIA 1987); *Matter of Guerra*, 24 I&N Dec. 37 (BIA 2006).

[7] Average cost of detention is $95 a day. By contrast, alternatives to detention programs cost $10 to $14 a day. Response of Julie Myers to Senator Edward Kennedy's Questions on the Nomination to be Assistant Secretary of ICE (Oct. 3, 2007). Appearance rates for alternatives to detention programs: ICE Fact Sheet: Alternatives to Detention (March 16, 2009), *available at*

http://www.ice.gov/pi/news/factsheets/080115alternativestodetention.htm. *See also*, Vera Institute of Justice, *Testing Community Supervision for the INS: An Evaluation of the Appearance Assistance Program*, Volume 1 (Aug. 2000), Esther Ebrahimian, "The Ullin 22: Shelters and Legal Service Providers Offer Viable Alternatives to Detention," *Detention Watch Network News*, (Aug./Sept. 2000).

[8] Profiles are drawn from interviews Human Rights First conducted with detained and formerly detained refugees and pro bono attorneys in 2008 and 2009, unless otherwise noted.

[9] For additional information, please refer to the "Methodology" section in the full report.

[10] CRS Report for Congress, Immigration-Related Detention: Current Legislative Issues (April 28, 2004); Testimony of James T. Hayes, Jr., Director, Office of Detention and Removal Operations, "Hearing on Health Services for Detainees in ICE Custody," before the House Appropriations Committee Subcommittee on Homeland Security (March 3, 2009); Department of Homeland Security, "DHS Announces $12.4 Billion for Border Security & Immigration Enforcement" (Jan. 31, 2008), *available at* http://www.dhs.gov/xnews/releases/pr_1201803940204.shtm.

[11] See explanation of calculation of "48,000" number in endnote 4.

[12] See endnote 3.

[13] ICE, *Report to Congress: Detained Asylum Seekers Fiscal Year 2007* (2008).

[14] The U.S. Commission on International Religious Freedom was created by Congress through the International Religious Freedom Act of 1998 to provide data and independent policy recommendations to the President and Congress on religious repression and intolerance. The members of the Commission are experts in the fields relevant to the issue of international religious freedom and are appointed by the President and Congressional leaders from both parties. See www.uscirf.gov for additional information.

[15] U.S. Commission on International Religious Freedom, *Report on Asylum Seekers in Expedited Removal*, Vol. I, p. 68; UNHCR, *Guidelines on Detention of Asylum-Seekers* (Feb. 1999).

[16] ICE opened or began using the following detention facilities following the Commission's report: South Texas Detention Center (1,904 beds); Willacy Detention Center (3,000 beds); Stewart Detention Center (1,524 beds); T. Don Hutto Family Detention Center (512 beds); Bristol Detention Center (128 beds); LaSalle Detention Center (1,160 beds); Otero County Processing Center (1,088 beds).

[17] *See, e.g.* GAO, "Alien Detention Standards: Observations on the Adherence to ICE's Medical Standards in Detention Facilities," GAO-08-869T (June 2008); Dana Priest and Amy Goldstein, Washington Post, May 11, 2008; Nina Bernstein, "Few Details on Immigrants Who Die in Custody," New York Times (May 5, 2008); Department of Homeland Security, Office of Inspector General, Treatment of Immigration Detainees Housed at Immigration and Customs Enforcement Facilities," December 2006. Information on openings available at: Department of Homeland Security Division of Immigration Health Services, "Job Listings", (2009), available at https://jobs-dihs.icims.com/jobs/search?ss=1&searchKeyword=&searchLocation=&searchCategory=&searchRadius=5&searchZip=. Vacancy rate from testimony of Julie L. Myers, Assistant Secretary of U.S. Immigration and Customs Enforcement (ICE), "Hearing on Problems with Immigration Detainee Medical Care" (June 4, 2008). On detainee deaths, *see*, Testimony of Dora Schriro, "Hearing on Medical Care and Treatment of Immigration Detainees and Deaths in DRO Custody" (March 3, 2009); *see also* Dana Priest and Amy Goldstein, "Suicides Point to Gaps in Treatment" (May 13, 2008). On Failure to use interpreters, *see*, Dana Priest and Amy Goldstein, "Suicides Point to Gaps in Treatment" (May 13, 2008); *see also* Testimony of 'Asfaw', Refugee from Ethiopia who was given the wring medication without the use of an interpreter, "Hearing on Problems with Immigration Detainee Medical Care," (June 4, 2008).

[18] Testimony of Ann Schofield Baker, Pro Bono Attorney for Amina Mudey, McKool Smith, "Hearing on Problems with Immigration Detainee Medical Care," before House Judiciary Committee's Subcommittee on Immigration, Citizenship, Refugees, Border Security and International Law (June 4, 2008).

[19] Quote as reported to Human Rights First by representative of legal service provider in Arizona.

[20] See sections of report titled "Penal Detention Inappropriate Under International Standards," and "Arbitrary Detention Under International Law."

[21] International Covenant on Civil and Political Rights, 999 U.N.T.S. 171, (entered into force March 23, 1976). Article 9(4) of the International Covenant on Civil and Political Rights (ICCPR), to which the U.S. is a party, provides that all detained individuals shall be entitled to have the lawfulness of their detention reviewed by a court. The lack of such review renders the detention of arriving asylum seekers arbitrary. *See also* Human Rights First, Background Briefing Note: The Detention of Asylum Seekers in the United States: Arbitrary Under the ICCPR (Jan. 2007). The UNHCR Detention Guidelines call for procedural guarantees, when a decision to detain is made, including "automatic review before a judicial or administrative body independent of the detaining authorities." United Nations High Commissioner for Refugees (UNHCR), *Revised Guidelines on Applicable Criteria and Standards Relating to the Detention of Asylum-Seekers* (Feb. 1999); *See also* UNHCR, Executive Committee, *Conclusion on Detention of Refugees and Asylum Seekers*, No. 44 (1986).

[22] 8 CFR §1003.19 (h)(2)(i)(B). The majority of "arriving aliens" processed under expedited removal are not referred for credible fear interviews and are summarily removed.

[23] ICE, *Report to Congress: Detained Asylum Seekers Fiscal Year 2004* (2005); ICE, *Report to Congress: Detained Asylum Seekers Fiscal Year 2007* (2008).

[24] ICE, "Parole of Arriving Aliens Found to Have a 'Credible Fear'" (Nov. 6, 2007).

[25] ICE, *Report to Congress: Detained Asylum Seekers Fiscal Year 2007* (2008) (showing an average length of detention of 93.8 days for asylum seekers detained in fiscal year 2007). By comparison, the average length of detention for immigration detainees overall was 26.9 days in fiscal year 2007. ICE, *Fact Sheet: Detention Management* (Nov. 20, 2008), available at http://www.ice.gov/pi/news/factsheets/detention_mgmt.htm.

[26] Profiles are drawn from interviews Human Rights First conducted with formerly detained refugees and legal service providers, including those conducted in 2008 and 2009 in preparation for this report.

[27] Physicians for Human Rights and the Bellevue/NYU Program for Survivors of Torture, *From Persecution to Prison: The Health Consequences of Detention for Asylum Seekers* (June 2003).

[28] *Gomez-Zuluaga v. AG of the United States,* 527 F.3d 330, 339 (3rd Cir. 2008).

[29] Response of Julie Myers to Senator Edward Kennedy's Questions on the Nomination to be Assistant Secretary of ICE (Oct. 3, 2007).

[30] Leslie Berestein, "Detention Dollars: Tougher Immigration Laws Turn the Ailing Private Prison Sector Into a Revenue Maker," *The San Diego Union-Tribune* (May 4, 2008); ICE, "Fact Sheet: Fiscal Year 2009" (Oct. 23 2008), *available at* http://www.ice.gov/doclib/pi/news/factsheets/2009budgetfactsheet.doc. For calculation of overall cost and information on number of asylum seekers detained, see above endnote 4. Also see explanation in endnote 2 about 2007 statistics.

[31] Information on length of detention of the cases cited was obtained during Human Rights First interviews with formerly detained asylum seekers. Number of asylum seekers at the South Texas Detention Center and the and cost of detention at the New Jersey facility were provided by ICE. Cost of detention for the El Paso facility was calculated based on the average cost of detention for ICE Service Processing Centers ($119.28): Leslie Berestein, "Detention Dollars: Tougher Immigration Laws Turn the Ailing Private Prison Sector Into a Revenue Maker," *The San Diego Union-Tribune* (May 4, 2008). Cost of detention for the California facility: Anna Gorman, "Cities and Counties Rely on U.S. Immigrant Detention Fees," *Los Angeles Times* (March 17, 2009).

[32] EOIR, "Fact Sheet: EOIR's Video Conferencing Initiative" (Sept. 21, 2004); GAO, "Executive Office for Immigration Review: Caseload Performance Reporting Needs Improvement," GAO-06-771 (Aug. 2006), p 18; Frank M. Walsh and Edward M. Walsh, *Effective Processing or Assembly-Line Justice? The Use of Teleconferencing in Asylum Removal Hearings,* 22 Geo. Immigr. L.J. 259, 271 (2008).

[33] 2,723 out of 4,420 credible fear interviews conducted by video in 2007 – all from the Houston asylum office. Information provided by USCIS, at Asylum Office Headquarters liaison meeting (June 17, 2008 and March 9, 2009). Information on credible fear interview pass rates also provided by USCIS.

[34] These provisions are located primarily at 8 C.F.R. § 1003.19 and § 212.5, as well as § 208.30 and § 235.3.

[35] See, e.g., Florida Immigrant Advocacy Center, Dying for Decent Care: Bad Medicine in Immigration Custody (Feb. 2009); Human Rights Watch, Detained and Dismissed: Women's Struggles to Obtain Health Care in United States Immigration Detention (Feb. 2009); Amnesty International, Jailed Without Justice (March 2009); Physicians for Human Rights and The Bellevue/NYU Program for Survivors of Torture, From Persecution to Prison: The Health Consequences of Detention for Asylum Seekers (June 2003).

[36] U.N. Convention Relating to the Status of Refugees, 189 U.N.T.S. 137 (entered into force July 28, 1951); U.N. Protocol Relating to the Status of Refugees, 606 U.N.T.S. 268 (entered into force October 4, 1967). The United States acceded to the Refugee protocol in 1968 and incorporated its provisions into domestic law through the Refugee Act of 1980 Pub. L. No. 96-212, 94 Stat 102 (1980). As the Supreme Court has confirmed, a primary purpose of Congress in passing the Refugee Act "was to bring United States refugee law into conformance with the 1967 United Nations Protocol." *INS v. Cardoza-Fonseca,* 480 U.S. 421, 426 (1987); see also *INS v. Stevic,* 467 U.S. 407, 416-24 (1984) providing a history of the incorporation of the Refugee Convention standards into U.S. law through the Refugee Protocol and the Refugee Act of 1980.

[37] Statistics on affirmative asylum provided by USCIS Asylum Office; grant rate calculated by taking approvals out of cases adjudicated (approved, denied, or referred). Statistics on immigration court from U.S. Department of Justice, Executive Office for Immigration Review, "FY 2007 Statistical Year Book" (Falls Church: Office of Legislative and Public Affairs, 2008), p K2; grant rate calculated by taking grants out of cases adjudicated (grants and denials).

[38] For fiscal years 1975 through 2005, see Refugee Council USA, "U.S. Refugee Admission Program for Fiscal Year 2006 and 2007: the Impact of the Material Support Bar—Recommendations of Refugee Council USA," p. A-7; for fiscal years 2006 through 2009, see U.S. Department of State, "Refugee Processing Center" (2009), available at http://www.wrapsnet.org/Reports/AdmissionsArrivals/tabid/211/language/en-US/Default.aspx.

[39] Homeland Security Act of 2002, Section 101, available at http://www.whitehouse.gov/deptofhomeland/bill/.

[40] In November 2003, Human Rights First began urging DHS Secretary Thomas Ridge to create a high level of refugee protection in his office to ensure the proper resolution of refugee issues that cut across DHS bureaus Human Rights First Letter to Thomas J. Ridge (Nov. 5, 2003), *available at* http://www.humanrightsfirst.org/asylum/ridge_letter110503.pdf.

[41] USCIRF, *Asylum Seekers in Expedited Removal,* Vol. I, p. 64-65.

[42] USCIRF, *Asylum Seekers in Expedited Removal,* Vol. I, p. 51, 54, Vol. II, p. 14, 20; *See also* Eric Schmitt, "When Asylum Requests are Overlooked." *The New York Times,* August 15, 2001, at A6; John Moreno Gonzales, "Amityville Woman Seeks $8 Million in JFK Mix-Up," *Newsday,* July 12, 2000.

[43] DHS, Annual Report: Immigration Enforcement Actions: 2007 (Dec. 2008), *available at* http //www.dhs.gov/xlibrary/assets/statistics/publications/enforcement_ar_07.pdf.

[44] The U.S. Commission on International Religious Freedom recommended that DHS stop placing asylum seekers with valid visas into expedited removal and mandatory detention, but DHS did not implement this recommendation. USCIRF, *Asylum Seekers in Expedited Removal,* p. 69; Letter from Stewart Baker, Assistant Secretary of Policy DHS, to Felice Gaer, Chair of the U.S. Commission on International and Religious Freedom (Nov. 28, 2008).

[45] Testimony of Edwidge Danticat, before the House Judiciary Committee Subcommittee on Immigration, Citizenship, Refugees, Border Security, and International Law, "Hearing on Detention and Removal: Immigration Detainee Medical Care" (Oct. 4, 2007); Amy Goldstein and Dana Priest, "System of Neglect," Washington Post (May 11, 2008).

[46] Letter from Stewart Baker, Assistant Secretary of Policy DHS, to Felice Gaer, Chair of the U.S. Commission on International and Religious Freedom (Nov. 28, 2008).

[47] USCIRF, *Asylum Seekers in Expedited Removal*, p. 173.

[48] Information provided by USCIS Asylum Office.

[49] USCIRF, *Asylum Seekers in Expedited Removal*, p. 168.

[50] This rate is calculated as number of cases in which credible fear was found out of all credible fear decisions made (for 2008, credible fear was found in 3,128 cases out of 5,290 decisions made). Information provided by USCIS Asylum Office.

[51] In fiscal year 2007, for example, the Los Angeles asylum office had a pass rate of 54%; Statistics provided by USCIS Asylum Office.

[52] According to numbers received from the Asylum Office Headquarters, 8,469 individuals were found to have credible fear in the fiscal year 2005, 1,311 in fiscal year 2006, 3,182 in fiscal year 2007, 3,128 in fiscal year 2008, and 1,618 in the first five months of fiscal year 2009. According to government statistics included in USCIRF, *Asylum Seekers in Expedited Removal*, 7,241 individuals were found to have credible fear in fiscal year 2004. Because asylum seekers subject to the credible fear process are mandatorily detained, presumably all of these individuals were detained for at least some time.

[53] For example, according to an ICE report to Congress, in fiscal year 2004, 4,758 defensive asylum seekers and 165 affirmative asylum seekers were detained, and in 2006, 5,017 defensive asylum seekers and 487 affirmative asylum seekers were detained. ICE, *Report to Congress: Detained Asylum Seekers Fiscal Year 2004* (2005); ICE, *Report to Congress: Detained Asylum Seekers Fiscal Year 2006* (2007).

[54] According to ICE reports, 190 out of 56,120 affirmative asylum seekers were detained in fiscal year 2003 (0.34%); 165 out of 36,823 in fiscal year 2004 (0.45%), and 487 out of 22,983 in fiscal year 2006 (2.12%), and 254 of 24,908 in fiscal year 2007 (1.1%). Similar data has not been provided for fiscal years 2005, 2007, or 2008. ICE, *Report to Congress: Detained Asylum Seekers Fiscal Year 2003* (2004); ICE, *Report to Congress: Detained Asylum Seekers Fiscal Year 2004* (2005); ICE, *Report to Congress: Detained Asylum Seekers Fiscal Year 2006* (2007); ICE, *Report to Congress: Detained Asylum Seekers Fiscal Year 2007 (2008)*.

[55] Haitian Refugee Immigration Fairness Act of 1998, §§ 903-904, Pub. L. No. 105-277, 112 Stat. 2681-541 (codified at 8 U.S.C. §§ 1377-1378) (hereinafter Haitian Refugee Immigration Fairness Act).

[56] The total number of asylum seekers was obtained by adding the number of detained asylum seekers for the last seven months of fiscal year 2003 through February 2009. For years 2003, 2004, and 2006, the number of detained asylum seekers was obtained from ICE's section 903 reports under the Haitian Refugee and Immigration Fairness Act.(ICE, *Report to Congress: Detained Asylum Seekers Fiscal Year 2007 (2008)*; ICE, *Report to Congress: Detained Asylum Seekers Fiscal Year 2006* (2007); ICE, *Report to Congress: Detained Asylum Seekers Fiscal Year 2004* (2005); ICE, *Report to Congress: Detained Asylum Seekers Fiscal Year 2003* (2004)). They are 8,137, 11,909, 5,761, and 9,971 respectively. For 2005, 2008, and 2009 (through February), the number of detained asylum seekers was calculated by using the number of individuals who were found to have credible fear of persecution: 8,469 for fiscal year 2005, 3,128 for fiscal year 2008, and 1,618 for the first five months of fiscal year 2009 (credible fear statistics provided by U.S. Citizenship and Immigration Services). No data on the number of affirmative and defensive asylum seekers for these years has been made available by ICE.

[57] The regulations on parole state that aliens may only be paroled if "the aliens present neither a security risk nor a risk of absconding." 8 C.F.R. § 212.5. The most recent ICE guidelines on parole, as well as the previous guidance from 1997 and 1998, also provide that parole may only be considered for those who are not a flight or security risk. ICE, "Parole of Arriving Aliens Found to Have a 'Credible Fear'" (Nov. 6, 2007). Also , see, e.g., *Matter of Partel*, 15 I&N. Dec. 666 (BIA 1976); *Matter of Spiliopoulos*, 16 I&N Dec. 488 (BIA 1987); *Matter of Guerra*, 24 I&N Dec. 37 (BIA 2006).

[58] The average length of 93.8 was reported in 2007 – the last year for which this information was provided by ICE. ICE, *Report to Congress: Detained Asylum Seekers Fiscal Year 2007* (2008).

[59] USCIRF, *Expedited Removal Study Report Card: 2 Years Later* (Feb. 8, 2007), p. 5.

[60] U.S. Government Accountability Office, *DHS: Organizational Structure and Resources for Providing Health Care to Immigrant Detainees*, GAO-09-308R (Feb. 23, 2009), p.14.

[61] In its 2005 study on the detention of asylum seekers, the U.S. Commission on International Religious Freedom identified a variety of "attributes of confinement" that are characteristically found in jail settings. Among these are: housing unit counts; strip or other invasive searches; fixed guard stations in housing units; constant sight and sound surveillance; use of physical restraints; use of isolation; restriction on movements outside of housing unit;

escorts required when detainees move throughout facility; lack of privacy when using toilets and showers; inability to wear own clothing; restricted access to law library; inability to have contact visits. USCIRF, *Asylum Seekers in Expedited Removal*, Vol. II, p. 208-215.

[62] GAO, *DHS: Organizational Structure* (2009), p. 2.

[63] Id., p.14.

[64] USCIRF, *Asylum Seekers in Expedited Removal*, Vol. I, p. 63.

[65] Letter from Felice Gaer, Chair of USCIRF to Stewart Baker, Assistant Secretary for Policy DHS (Jan. 8, 2009).

[66] See chart below for list of new detention facilities opened in recent years.

[67] In November 2008, Human Rights First staff visited two county jails in rural Virginia where asylum seekers and other immigration detainees are held. During the visit, HRF staff had an opportunity to meet with facility staff, an ICE representative, and several detainees.

[68] ICE, *Report to Congress: Detained Asylum Seekers Fiscal Year 2006* (2007).

[69] Human Rights First interviewed scores of detained asylum seekers who have been handcuffed and shackled. For example, during a July 2007 tour of the Elizabeth Detention Center organized by Human Rights First and the American Friends Service Committee, ICE officials stated that detainees are handcuffed during initial detention and during any transfers. Asylum seekers may be handcuffed and shackled by Customs and Border Protection officers, if detained in a border area, by ICE officers, or by contractors hired by ICE to transport detainees to and from facilities.

[70] USCIRF, *Asylum Seekers in Expedited Removal*, Vol. II, p. 186.

[71] Seattle University School of Law and OneAmerica, *Voices From Detention: A Report on Human Rights Violations at the Northwest Detention Center* (June 2008), p. 7, 47.

[72] Over the years, Human Rights First has interviewed hundreds of asylum seekers who reported being handcuffed at the JFK and Newark airports and while transported to local detention facilities, including several interviewed for this report.

[73] Correspondence between Detention Watch Network members (Nov. 11, 2008).

[74] ICE Detention Standard, "Use of Force," (Sept. 20, 2000); see also, ICE/DRO Detention Standard, "Use of Force and Restraints" (Dec. 2008).

[75] USCIRF, *Asylum Seekers in Expedited Removal*, Vol. II, p. 186.

[76] Physicians for Human Rights, *From Persecution to Prison* (June 2003) p. 191.

[77] USCIRF, *Asylum Seekers in Expedited Removal*, Vol. II, p. 185.

[78] Interview with an asylum seeker detained at the Elizabeth Detention Center for four months (August 2008).

[79] USCIRF, *Asylum Seekers in Expedited Removal*, Vol. II, p. 185.

[80] Seattle University School of Law, *Voices from Detention*, p. 56.

[81] Senator Menendez of New Jersey and Lutheran Bishop Riley visited the facility in July 2008.

[82] Tricia Lynn Silva, "New detention center sign of Pearsall's biz-friendly outreach." *San Antonio Business Journal*, March 5, 2004, *available at* http://www.bizjournals.com/sanantonio/stories/2004/03/08/story5.html.

[83] During a tour of the facility in November 2008, Human Rights First staff was informed that the recreation area available at this facility is in fact not considered outdoor, and that this creates limitations on how long detainees may remain at the facility. Human Rights First staff, has however, spoken to a number of asylum seekers and other detainees who have spent several months at this facility.

[84] ICE Detention Standard, "Recreation" (Sep. 20, 2000), *available at* http://www.ice.gov/doclib/partners/dro/opsmanual/recreat.pdf. The new "Performance Based Standards," which were released in September 2008 and are in the process of being implemented, state that "It is expected that every ICE/DRO detainee will be placed in a facility that provides indoor and outdoor recreation. However, in exceptional circumstances, a facility lacking outdoor recreation or any recreation area may be used to provide short-term housing;" and provides—similarly to the Detention Standards—that detainees held at facilities without an outdoor recreation space may request a transfer after six months. It is also worth noting that the new standards state that all new contracts with detention centers or local facilities "shall stipulate that ICE/DRO detainees have access to an outdoor recreation area." ICE/DRO Detention Standard, "Recreation" (Dec. 2, 2008), *available at* http://www.ice.gov/doclib/PBNDS/pdf/recreation.pdf.

[85] Women's Commission for Refugee Women and Children and the Lutheran Immigration and Refugee Service, *Locking Up Family Values: The Detention of Immigrant Families* (Feb. 2007), p. 27.

[86] Visit to the detention center by Human Rights First staff (May 2008); Conversations with local legal service providers (May 2008).

[87] See ICE, "Immigration Detention Facilities," *at* http://www.ice.gov/pi/dro/facilities.htm.

[88] USCIRF, *Asylum Seekers in Expedited Removal,* Vol. I, p 60.

[89] USCIRF, *Asylum Seekers in Expedited Removal,* Vol. I, p. 69.

[90] USCIRF, *Report Card;* see also USCIRF, *Asylum Seekers in Expedited Removal.* The new "Performance Based Standards" that were issued by ICE in September 2008 continue to rely on correctional standards. In fact, the standards cite to the American Correctional Association standards for adult facilities as a reference. The Commission, in a January 2009 letter to DHS, wrote that they "do not believe that these [Performance Based] standards address our concerns or recommendations...[they] rely on correctional standards, which are inappropriate for asylum seekers." (USCIRF, "USCIRF disappointed that DHS action on expedited removal process falls short" (Jan. 9, 2009), *available at* http://www.uscirf.gov/index.php?option=com_content&task=view&id=2340&Itemid=126).

[91] USCIRF, *Asylum Seekers in Expedited Removal,* Vol. II, p. 189; USCIRF, *Report Card,* p. 5.

[92] USCIRF, *Asylum Seekers in Expedited Removal,* Vol. I, p. 68.

[93] Id., Vol. II, p. 200 and Vol. I, p. 61.

[94] USCIRF, *Report Card,* p. 5.

[95] See, e.g. Florida Immigrant Advocacy Center, *Dying for Decent Care: Bad Medicine in Immigration Custody* (March 2009), *available at* http://www.fiacfla.org/reports/DyingForDecentCare.pdf. See also Luis Perez, "Detained Immigrants in Florida complain they're not getting medical care," *South Florida Sun Sentinel* (March 17, 2009) *available at* http://www.sun-sentinel.com/news/local/broward/sfl-flbdetainhealth0317pnmar17,0,1027089.story.

[96] DHS, "DHS Announces $12.4 Billion for Border Security and Immigration Enforcement" (Jan. 31, 2008).

[97] Fernando Del Valle, "Willacy to Expand Detention Center," *Valley Morning Star* (July 25, 2007), *available at* http://www.valleymorningstar.com/news/detention_6898___article.html/center_barnhart.html.

[98] Detention Watch Network, "Stewart Detention Center" (Dec. 8, 2008) at http://www.detentionwatchnetwork.org/stewart.

[99] ICE, *The ICE T. Don Hutto Family Residential Facility: Maintaining Family Unity, Enforcing Immigration Laws* (April 2007), *available at* http://www.ice.gov/pi/news/factsheets/huttofactsheet.htm.

[100] GEO Group, Northwest Detention Center, *available at* http://www.thegeogroupinc.com/northamerica.asp?fid=105.

[101] Aaron Nicodemus, "New Dartmouth jail facility to house illegal immigrants," *The Standard-Times* (April 2, 2007), *available at* http://www.southcoasttoday.com/apps/pbcs.dll/article?AID=/20070402/NEWS/704020337/-1/SPECIAL21.

[102] GEO Group, LaSalle Detention Facility, *available at* http://www.thegeogroupinc.com/northamerica.asp?fid=120.

[103] Bryan Gibel, "Immigration advocates say prison expansion will only compound problems," *The Santa-Fe New Mexican* (Mar. 17, 2008), *available at* http://www.santafenewmexican.com/SantaFeNorthernNM/otero-county-More-detainees--more-complaints.

[104] Josh White and Nick Miroff, "The Profit of Detention," *Washington Post,* (Oct. 5, 2008), *available at* http://www.washingtonpost.com/wp-dyn/content/article/2008/10/04/AR2008100402434.html; *see also* Tim Craig, "Immigrant Detention Centre Propsed in Va.," *Washington Post* (Sep. 26, 2007), *available at* http://www.washingtonpost.com/wp-dyn/content/article/2007/09/25/AR2007092502190.html; Jamie C. Ruff, "Immigrant Holding Facility to be Built in Va.," *Richmond Times-Dispatch Online (inrich.com)* (Sep. 29, 2008), *available at* http://www.inrich.com/cva/ric/news.apx.-content-articles-RTD-2008-09-29-0133.html.

[105] Anna Gorman, "Immigration Detention Center Considered for L.A. Area," *Los Angeles Times* (Feb. 3, 2009), *available at* http://www.latimes.com/news/printedition/california/la-me-ladetain3-2009feb03,0,3449452.story.

[106] "Area's 2nd immigration holding centre proposed in Mustang Ridge," *KLBJ News Radio Newsroom,* (Mar. 21, 2008), *available at* http://www.590klbj.com/News/Story.aspx?ID=87343.

[107] Adam Goldstein, "Expansion Approved for Private Detention Center," The Aurora Sentinel (Apr. 16, 2008).

[108] GEO Group, "The GEO Group, Inc. Signs Contract with Maverick County, Texas for the Development and Operation of a 654-Bed Detention Facility," (

[109] *See* DHS Solicitation for Contractor-Owned, Contractor-Operated Detention Facility of 1,575 beds, *available at* https://www.fbo.gov/index?s=opportunity&mode=form&id=8bd8a9dc40d4213623206d94d21777e4&tab=core&_cview=0),

[110] Stephen Gurr, "Main Street jail renovations waiting on local, federal agreement," *Gainesville Times.com* (Mar. 4, 2009), *available at* http://www.gainesvilletimes.com/news/archive/15685/; *see also* Associated Press, "Old Hall jail getting upgrade, new name," *The Atlanta Journal-Constitution Online,* (Dec. 16, 2008), *available at* http://www.ajc.com/services/content/printedition/2008/12/16/halljail.html?cxntlid=inform_sr;

Associated Press, "Corrections Corp to manage Georgia facility" (March 9, 2009), *available at* http://www.forbes.com/feeds/ap/2009/03/09/ap6143793.html.

[111] Department of Homeland Security, "DHS Announces $12.4 Billion for Border Security & Immigration Enforcement" (Jan. 31, 2008), *available at* http://www.dhs.gov/xnews/releases/pr_1201803940204.shtm.

[112] Testimony of Dora Schriro, Special Advisor on Detention and Removal Operations, before the House Appropriations Committee Subcommittee on Homeland Security, "Hearing on Medical Care and Treatment of Immigration Detainees and Deaths in DRO Custody" (March 3, 2009).

[113] See chart outlining pending proposals for additional detention bed space.

[114] Information obtained during Human Rights First tour of the facility (May 2008).

[115] Correspondence between pro bono attorneys who represent clients at the facility and Human Rights First (Jan. 2009).

[116] Correspondence between Willacy Detention Center and Human Rights First (Sept. 2008).

[117] CCA Source, "CCA Opens Stewart Detention Center," *available at* http://www.ccasource.com/story.cfm?d=307.

[118] Conversation with representative from Catholic Charities of Atlanta and the American Civil Liberties Union of Georgia (Feb. 2009).

[119] During the summer and fall of 2008, a handful of detainees at the Elizabeth Detention Center in New Jersey have told Human Rights First staff conducting legal orientation presentations at the facility that they were originally detained in New Jersey and then transferred to Georgia or a jail in Alabama, where they spent several weeks or even months before being returned to detention in New Jersey. Local ICE officers in New Jersey have responded to inquiries from attorneys and family members of transferred detainees by explaining that the Elizabeth Detention Center does not have the capacity to detain long-term detainees, and that these detainees are transferred elsewhere to make room for new arrivals. Detainees then seem to be returned to New Jersey in preparation for their removal. (Conversations with family members and attorneys).

[120] Conversation with representative from Catholic Charities of Atlanta (Feb. 2009).

[121] Seattle University School of Law, *Voices from Detention*, p 6 & 51.

[122] Id., p. 57.

[123] Id., p. 36.

[124] GAO, *DHS: Organizational Structure*, p.14.

[125] U.S. Department of Justice, Bureau of Justice Statistics, "Table 6.61.2006, Detainees under Bureau of Immigration and Customs Enforcement (ICE) jurisdiction," *Sourcebook of Criminal Justice Statistics Online*, *available at* http://www.albany.edu/sourcebook/pdf/t6612006.pdf.

[126] Justice Policy Institute, *Jailing Communities: The impact of jail expansion and effective public safety strategies* (Washington D.C: Justice Policy Institute, April 2008), *available at* http://www.justicepolicy.org/images/upload/08-04_REP_JailingCommunities_AC.pdf; GAO, *DHS: Organizational Structure*, 2009, p. 15.

[127] Correspondence between pro bono attorneys from Advocates for Human Rights in Minnesota and the National Immigrant Justice Center in Chicago, Illinois, and Human Rights First (March 2009).

[128] House Committee on Appropriations, Department of Homeland Security appropriations bill, 2006: report together with additional views (to accompany H.R. 2360), 109th Cong., 1st Session, 2005, H. Rep. 109-79. *See also* Women's Refugee Commission, *Locking Up Family Values*, p. 5-6.

[129] ICE, "The ICE T.Don Hutto Family Residential Facility: maintaining family unity, enforcing immigration laws,' (Apr. 2007), *available at* http://www.ice.gov/pi/news/factsheets/huttofactsheet.htm.

[130] According to ICE's *Report to Congress: Detained Asylum Seekers Fiscal Year 2006* (2007), in fiscal year 2006, 105 asylum seekers were detained at the Hutto facility. An additional 61 were detained at the Berks County family detention center. However, see Human Rights First's concerns on these statistics in prior endnote. *See also* Women's Commission, *Locking Up Family Values*: "Although the majority of the families are nationals of Central or South American countries, a review of the total population statistics indicated that there were also detainees from Djibouti, Ethiopia, Greece, Haiti, Indonesia, Iraq, Jordan, Kuwait, Romania an Somalia. Many of these families had been apprehended along the U.S.-Mexico border and are in expedited removal proceedings, however there were also families who were apprehended in the interior as well as many asylum seekers." p. 11.

[131] Women's Refugee Commission, *Locking Up Family Values*, p. 16-17.

[132] *See, e.g.* Ralph Blumenthal, "U.S. Gives Tour of Family Detention Center That Critics Liken to a Prison," *New York Times*, Feb. 19, 2007, *available at* http://www.nytimes.com/2007/02/10/us/10detain.html?_r=2/; Margaret Talbot, "The Lost children: What Do Tougher Detention Policies Mean for Illegal Immigrant Families?," The New Yorker (March 3, 2008).

[133] Women's Refugee Commission, *Locking Up Family Values*, p. 25.

[134] American Civil Liberties Union, "*ACLU Challenges Prison-Like Conditions at Hutto Detention Center*," available at http://www.aclu.org/immigrants/detention/hutto.html; *Correspondence between representatives of the Women's Refugee Commission and Human Rights First* (April 2009).

[135] Correspondence between Barbara Hines, Clinical Professor of Law, University of Texas School of Law and Human Rights First (Apr. 2009).

[136] Women's Refugee Commission, *Locking Up Family Values*, p. 17.

[137] UNHCR, *Refugee Children: Guidelines on Protection and Care* (Geneva: UNHCR, 1994), available at http://www.unhcr.org/cgi-bin/texis/vtx/protect/opendoc.pdf?tbl=PROTECTION&id=3b84c6c67.

[138] The August 2007 settlement led to the release of several families, including dozens of children, and imposed a requirement on ICE to conduct a review of a family's detention within 30 days of the initial detention. (Settlement Agreement, *In re Hutto Family Detention Centre*, Case No. A-07-CA-164-SS, U.S. District Court Western District of Texas (August 26, 2007), *available at* http://www.aclutx.org/files/Hutto%20Settlement%20Agreement.pdf.)

[139] National Immigrant Justice Center, "ICE Accepts NGO Recommendations on Family Detention Standards; But More Progress Is Needed" (Jan. 18, 2008), *available at* http://www.immigrantjustice.org/index.php?option=com_content&task=view&id=300&Itemid=93.

[140] Women's Refugee Commission, "New Family Detention Standards Incorporate Women's Commission's Recommendations on treatment of Immigrant and Refugee Families: Women's Commission Calls Standards a 'step in the right direction'" (Jan. 11, 2008), *available at* http://www.womenscommission.org/pdf/pr_famdeten1.pdf. *See also* National Immigrant Justice Center, "ICE Accepts NGO Recommendations;" Women's Commission for Refugee Women and Children, "The Women's Commission Calls on ICE to Follow Congressional Directives on Family Detention" (June 12, 2008), *available at* http://www.womenscommission.org/pdf/statementRFP.pdf.

[141] Anna Gorman, "Immigration Agency Plans New Family Detention Centers," *Los Angeles Times*, May 18, 2008, *available at* http://articles.latimes.com/2008/may/18/nation/na-detention18.

[142] Department of Homeland Security advertising on Federal Business Opportunities.gov, "This Pre-solicitation is for non-criminal family residential facility" (Apr. 1, 2008), *available at* https://www.fbo.gov/index?s=opportunity&mode=form&id=5045f25a22246a27f29e75d279ba9762&tab=core&_cview=1&cck=1&au=&ck.

[143] Women's Refugee Commission, "New Family Detention Standards." *See also* National Immigrant Justice Center, "ICE Accepts NGO Recommendations."

[144] U.N. Convention Relating to the Status of Refugees (entered into force July 28, 1951); U.N. Protocol Relating to the Status of Refugees (entered into force October 4, 1967).

[145] UNHCR Executive Committee, *Conclusion No. 44* (1986).

[146] UNHCR, *Guidelines on Detention of Asylum-Seekers* (Feb. 1999). The Guidelines urge that exceptions to this general rule (protection of national security and public order, verification of identity, identification of basis of claim in a preliminary interview, destruction of documents/use of fraudulent documents to mislead) be clearly prescribed by national law in conformity with principles of international law.

[147] Arriving asylum seekers are subject to "mandatory detention" until they are found to have a credible fear of persecution, at which point they may be considered for release on parole. See, 8 C.F.R. § 235.3(b)(9).

[148] 8 C.F.R. § 212.5; 8 C.F.R. 1008.19

[149] In the last six years, U.S. immigration authorities have detained asylum seekers who arrive on valid passports and visas.

[150] 8 C.F.R. § 212.5; ICE, "Parole of Arriving Aliens Found to Have a 'Credible Fear'" (Nov. 6, 2007).

[151] ICE, "Parole of Arriving Aliens Found to Have a 'Credible Fear'" (Nov. 6, 2007).

[152] Article 9(4) of the *International Covenant on Civil and Political Rights* (ICCPR) (entered into force on March 23, 1976), to which the U.S. is a party, provides that all detained individuals shall be entitled to have the lawfulness of their detention reviewed by a court. The lack of such review renders the detention of arriving asylum seekers arbitrary. The UNHCR Guidelines call for procedural guarantees when a decision to detain is made, including "automatic review before a judicial or administrative body independent of the detaining authorities." UNHCR, *Guidelines on Detention of Asylum-Seekers* (1999), *See also* UNHCR Executive Committee, *Conclusion No. 44* (1986).

[153] 8 CFR §1003.19 (h)(2)(i)(B).

[154] ICCPR article 9(4).

[155] See *A. v. Australia*, United Nations Human Rights Committee (Apr. 30, 1997).

[156] UNHCR Executive Committee, *Conclusion No. 44*.

[157] UNHCR, *Guidelines on Detention of Asylum-Seekers*.

[158] UN Human Rights Council, *Report of the Special Rapporteur on the Human Rights of Migrants, Jorge Bustamante: Mission to the United States of America* (5 March 2008) A/HRC/7/12/Add.2.

[159] See e.g. Nadarajah v Gonzalez 443 F.3d 1069, 1075 (9th Cir. 2006) (federal district court's denial of a habeas petition issued one year after asylum seeker filed petition).

[160] *See Veerikathy v INS*, 98 Civ. 2591, 1998 U.S. Dist. LEXIS 19360 (E.D.N.Y. Oct. 9, 1998); *see also Bertrand v. Sava* 684 F.2d 204 (2d Cir. 1982); *Zhang v. Slattery*, 840 F. Supp. 292 (S.D.N.Y. 1994); Nadarajah v Gonzalez 443 F.3d 1069, 1075 (9th Cir. 2006) (if a "facially legitimate and bona fide" reason for denying parole is provided, the "denial of parole is essentially unreviewable." Finding agency abused its discretion in denying parole because the reasons it provided were not facially legitimate and bona fde.)

[161] USCIRF, *Asylum Seekers in Expedited Removal*, Vol. II, p. 332.

[162] USCIRF, *Asylum Seekers in Expedited Removal*, Vol. I, p. 62, *see also* USCIRF, *Report Card*, p. 5.

[163] Id., p. 67.

[164] USCIRF, *Report Card*, summary p. 2.

[165] ICE, "Parole of Arriving Aliens Found to Have a 'Credible Fear.'"

[166] Memorandum by Michael A. Pearson, Executive Associate Commissioner for Field Operations (Dec. 30, 1997); Memorandum by Michael A. Pearson, Executive Associate Commissioner Officer of Field Operations (Oct. 7, 1998).

[167] ICE, "Parole of Arriving Aliens Found to Have a 'Credible Fear,'" § 4.

[168] Letter from Julie L. Myers, Assistant Secretary of ICE, to Eleanor Acer, Director of the Refugee Protection Program, Human Rights First (Dec. 3, 2007).

[169] Memorandum by Michael A. Pearson, Executive Associate Commissioner for Field Operations (Dec. 30, 1997); Memorandum by Michael A. Pearson, Executive Associate Commissioner Officer of Field Operations (Oct. 7, 1998).

[170] Prior criteria stated that parole considerations are "critical," and the district director should review the credible fear interview records and any accompanying information to make a parole determination. Memorandum by Michael A. Pearson, Executive Associate Commissioner for Field Operations (Dec. 30, 1997). A 2004 memorandum by the Acting Director of ICE, also stated that "Once credible fear is found, each case must be individually reviewed under these custody criteria." Memorandum by Victor X. Cerda, Acting Director of ICE (Sept. 14, 2004).The new parole directive states: "Upon receipt of a written INA § 212(d)(5) parole request by an arriving alien found to have a 'credible fear' of persecution or torture, the receiving DRO Field Office shall assign the request to a DRO officer...who will complete the ICE *Record of Determination/Parole Determination Worksheet*." I.C.E, "Parole of Arriving Aliens Found to Have a 'Credible Fear,'" § 8.1.

[171] Statistics for fiscal year 2008 on representation for detained and non-detained asylum seekers provided in correspondence from the Executive Office of Immigration Review to Human Rights First (Feb. 25, 2009).

[172] The U.S. Commission on International Religious Freedom, in its 2005 report, found wide variations across the country in parole rates, and concluded that there is "no evidence that ICE is consistently applying release criteria." USCIRF, *Asylum Seekers in Expedited Removal*, Vol. I, p. 62. *See also*, Human Rights First, *In Liberty's Shadow: U.S. Detention of Asylum Seekers in the Era of Homeland Security* (2004), p. 13.

[173] USCIRF, "USCIRF Expresses Concern to DHS over new policy directive on asylum seekers" (Dec. 14, 2007), *available at* http://www.uscirf.gov/index.php?option=com_content&task=view&id=45&Itemid=47.

[174] Letter from Felice Gaer, Chair of U.S. Commission on International Religious Freedom to Stewart Baker, Assistant Secretary of Policy DHS (Jan. 8, 2009).

[175] National Immigrant Justice Center, "ICE Policy that denies liberty to asylum seekers must be rescinded" (Nov. 16, 2007), *available at* http://www.immigrantjustice.org/resources/policy/asylum/Nov2007paroledirective.html; Hebrew Immigrant Aid Society, "Department of Homeland Security (DHS) Issues New Asylum Policy; More Likely That Victims of Persecution Will Remain in Jail" (Nov. 14, 2007), *available at* http://www.hias.org/news/department-homeland-security-dhs-issues-new-asylum-policy; Sign-on letter by 82 non-governmental organizations and experts, Feb. 19, 2008, *available at http://www.humanrightsfirst.info/pdf/rp-letter-parole.pdf*.

[176] USCIRF, *Asylum Seekers in Expedited Removal*, Vol. II, p. 333. The rate of release dropped from 86.1% in fiscal year 2001, to 62.5% in fiscal year 2003 for asylum seekers placed into expedited removal and found to have a credible fear of persecution.

[177] ICE, *Report to Congress: Detained Asylum Seekers Fiscal Year 2007* (2008).

[178] Letter from Stewart Baker, Assistant Secretary of Policy. DHS, to Felice Gaer, Chair of the U.S. Commission on International and Religious Freedom (Nov. 28, 2008).The number of arriving asylum seekers who were found to have credible fear in November 2007 through June 2008 was provided by the USCIS Asylum Office to Human Rights First.

[179] DHS/ICE did not report how many asylum seekers were newly detained during that time period, or how many asylum seekers overall were in detention during that time period (Letter from Stewart Baker, Assistant Secretary of Policy, DHS, to Felice Gaer, Chair of the U.S. Commission on International and Religious Freedom (Nov. 28, 2008).

[180] Correspondence between representative from Florida Immigrant Advocacy Center and Human Rights First (Nov. 2008).

[181] Correspondence between representative form National Immigrant Justice Center and Human Rights First (Feb. 2009).

[182] Correspondence between representative from the Immigration Clinic at the University of Texas Law School and Human Rights First (Oct. 2008).

[183] Correspondence between attorney Jodi Goodwin and Human Rights First (Oct. 2008).

[184] Correspondence between Human Rights First and a representative from American Gateways (Nov. 2008).

[185] Correspondence between Human Rights First and a representative from the Capital Area Immigrants' Rights Coalition (Oct. 2008).

[186] Interview with representative from a pro bono legal organization in Arizona. (May 2008).

[187] Correspondence between representative from American Gateways (formerly known as the Political Asylum Project of Austin) and Human Rights First (Feb. 2009).

[188] Correspondence between individual's attorney and Human Rights First (March 2009).

[189] Conversation between representative from RAICES and Human Rights First (May 2008), and follow-up correspondence (Feb. 2009).

[190] Correspondence between pro bono attorneys in Arizona, Massachusetts, and Texas and Human Rights First (Feb. 2009).

[191] "The determination of the Immigration Judge as to custody status or bond may be based upon any information that is available to the Immigration Judge or that is presented to him or her by the alien or the Service." 8 CFR § 1003.19(d). The factors to be considered in setting an immigration bond were set out in *Matter of Patel*, 15 I&N Dec. 666 (BIA 1976): "We have held that an alien generally should not be detained or required to post bond pending a determination of deportability unless there is a finding that he is a threat to the national security or is a poor bail risk." The BIA went on to consider the alien's criminal record and community ties, among other factors.

[192] Immigration and Nationality Act § 236(a)(2) (8 U.S.C. § 1226(a)(2)).

[193] ICE, "Open Bond Files at ICE Field Offices," provided in correspondence from ICE to Human Rights First (Jan. 16, 2009). Details average bond amounts by ICE Field Office for January 2009.

[194] ICE, *Report to Congress: Detained Asylum Seekers Fiscal Year 2004* (2005); ICE, *Report to Congress: Detained Asylum Seekers Fiscal Year 2007* (2008).

[195] Correspondence between representative of Catholic Charities of Austin and Human Rights First (Nov. 2008, Feb. 2009).

[196] While the U.S. Supreme Court has recognized that indefinite detention would raise serious due process concerns under the U.S. Constitution, and has held that the indefinite detention of persons subject to final orders of removal violates the immigration statute, the U.S. Department of Justice has argued that these holdings are limited to cases involving final orders of removal. See Zadvydas v. Davis, 533 U.S. 678 (2001) (holding in case of persons who previously entered the U.S. that statutory provision governing detention after final order of removal, read in light of the Constitution's requirements, does not permit indefinite detention); Clark v. Martinez, 543 U.S. 371 (2005) (applying the same holding to persons who have not been admitted to the U.S.); Nadarajah v. Gonzales 443 F.3d 1069, 1075 (9th Cir. 2006) (holding, contrary to government's position, that general detention statutes do not authorize indefinite detention of non-citizens whose claims for asylum or other relief are still pending).

[197] Haitian Refugee Immigration Fairness Act § 903.

[198] USCIRF, *Asylum Seekers in Expedited Removal*, Vol. II, p. 75.

[199] ICE, *Report to Congress: Detained Asylum Seekers Fiscal Year 2006* (2007).

[200] ICE, *Report to Congress: Detained Asylum Seekers Fiscal Year 2007* (2008).

[201] Physicians for Human Rights, *From Persecution to Prison* (June 2003), p. 2.

[202] Michelle Roberts, Associated Press, "Immigrants Face Long Detention, Few Rights," *International Herald Tribune* (Mar. 15, 2009).

[203] American Civil Liberties Union, "Court Says 'No' to Indefinite Detention" (Mar. 17, 2006) reports on a Sri Lankan asylum seeker detained for nearly five years; *Matter of S-K*, 231.& N. Dec. 936 (BIA 2006), in which a Burmese woman seeking asylum was detained for two and a half years in El Paso, Texas; Nina Bernstein, "Out of Repression, Into Jail; Detention for Asylum Seekers Is Routine, but U.S. is Taking Another Look," *New York Times* (Jan. 15, 2004); T. Knapp, "Freedom: Release" *Intelligencer Journal* (Jan. 17, 2008) reports on a Coptic Christian from Egypt who spent eight years in various detention

centers before being granted relief under the Convention Against Torture; Michelle Roberts, Associated Press, "Immigrants Face Long Detention, Few Rights," *International Herald Tribune* (Mar. 15, 2009).

[204] Correspondence between Human Rights First and Jay Sparks, Assistant Field Office Director at the Pearsall facility, and Andrew Strait, Acting Coordinator/Policy Analyst, National Community Outreach Program (Sep. 2008).

[205] See more complete profile later in this report.

[206] Interviews with pro bono practitioners in Arizona and Florida (Mar. 2008).

[207] Correspondence between Florence Immigrant and Refugee Rights Project and Human Rights First.

[208] Memorandum by Michael J. Garcia, Assistant Secretary of ICE, "Detention Policy Where an Immigration Judge has Granted Asylum and ICE has Appealed" (Feb. 9, 2004).

[209] ICE, "Parole of Arriving Aliens Found to Have a 'Credible Fear,'" § 3.

[210] Detention Watch Network and American Immigration Law Foundation, *Minutes of Meeting* (June 28, 2008); Correspondence between Human Rights First and pro bono providers in Arizona and Florida (Feb. 2009).

[211] Interviews and e-mail correspondence with pro bono attorneys from Arizona (March 2008), and Florida (March 2008 and February 2009). The regulations provide that someone granted withholding of removal under § 241(b)93)(B) of the Immigration and Nationality Act or withholding of removal under the Convention Against Torture may still be removed to a third country. See 8 CFR § 208.16(f).

[212] Haitian Refugee and Immigration Fairness Act §903.

[213] ICE's statistics appear to indicate that only 257 asylum seekers were detained under expedited removal. (ICE, *Report to Congress: Detained Asylum Seekers Fiscal Year 2006* (2007)). Yet during that same year, at least 3,320 asylum seekers were subject to expedited removal (and its mandatory detention provisions) and found to meet the credible fear screening standard. (Statistics found in "Credible Fear Workload Report for fiscal year 2006", provided in correspondence from the Asylum Office Headquarters to Human Rights First (Nov.2006)). At another point however, the statistics state that the "257" number reflects the number of asylum seekers who were detained initially during 2006, *and released* by the time the statistical report was generated in March 2007. If that is the case, then it may in fact be that only 16 asylum seekers (out of the 257 who were initially detained during 2006 and released by the time the report was generated) were released on parole. After reviewing these statistics, Human Rights First advised ICE of its questions regarding the statistics.

[214] These reports appear to include information only on those asylum seekers who were initially detained during the fiscal year being reported on. Therefore, the length of detention of asylum seekers detained in previous years and who continue to be detained during the fiscal year that is the basis of the report are not calculated.

[215] Physicians for Human Rights, *From Persecution to Prison* (June 2003).

[216] Because the INS was unwilling to provide open access to the detention facilities, the sample group of detained asylum seekers was obtained by contacting attorneys and other representatives who could identify specific detainees willing to participate in the study. *Id.* at 45. 51.

[217] *Id.* at 11, 51.

[218] *Id.* at 56-57.

[219] *Id.* at 58, 73-74, and 66-67.

[220] Physicians for Human Rights, *From Persecution to Prison* (June 2003).

[221] Derrick Silove, Patricia Austin & Zachary Steel, "No Refuge from Terror: The Impact of Detention on the Mental Health of Trauma-affected Refugees Seeking Asylum in Australia" *Transcultural Psychiatry*, Vol. 44, No. 3, 359 (2007); Mina Fazei & Derrick Silove, "Detention of Refugees" *British Medical Journal*, February 4, 2006, *available at* http://www.bmj.com/cgi/content/full/332/7536/251; Zachary Steel et al., "Impact of Immigration Detention and Temporary Protection on the Mental Health of Refugees," *The British Journal of Psychiatry* (2006) 188: 58-64; Testimony of Allen S. Keller, MD, "Hearing on Detention and Removal: Immigration Detainee Medical Care," before the House Judiciary Committee's Subcommittee on Immigration, Citizenship, Refugees, Border Security, and International Law (October 4 2007). .

[222] Zachary Steel et al., "Impact of Immigration Detention," *The British Journal of Psychiatry* (2006) 188.

[223] USCIRF, *Asylum Seekers in Expedited Removal*, Vol. I, p. 4, and Vol. II, p. 197.

[224] See, e.g. Donald Kerwin, "Due process for immigrants" (May 2008), *available at* http://www.ilw.com/articles/2008,0723-kerwin.shtm.

[225] Statistics provided by EOIR in correspondence with Human Rights First (Feb. 25, 2009).

[226] Jaya Ramji Nogales, Andrew Schoenholtz and Phillip Schrag, *Refugee Roulette: Disparities in asylum adjudication*, 60 Stan. L. Rev. 295, 340 (2007).

[227] Statistics provided in correspondence between EOIR and Human Rights First (Feb. 25, 2009).

[228] Vera Institute of Justice, *Legal Orientation Program: Evaluation and Performance and Outcome Measurement Report,* Phase II (New York: Vera Institute of Justice, May 2008), p. 63 (29% of detained LOP participants who had filed an I-589 were represented, as opposed to 71% of LOP participants who had filed an I-589 and had been released from detention).

[229] USCIRF, *Asylum Seekers in Expedited Removal,* Vol. II, p. 239 ("Detained asylum seekers who are not conversant in English may have difficulty finding legal counsel, even more difficulty conducting legal research and representing themselves in immigration court.") *See also,* Letter from UNHCR Regional Representative, to Senator Spencer Abraham, Senate Sub-Committee on Immigration (Sept. 15, 1998).

[230] *See, e.g.* Michele Pistone, "Justice Delayed is Justice Denied: A Proposal for Ending the Unnecessary Detention of Asylum Seekers," *Harvard Human Rights Journal,* Vol. 12, Spring 1999, at 219-220.

[231] ICE, "Detention Operations Manual INS Detention Standard: Telephone Access" (Sept. 20, 2000), *available at* http://www.ice.gov/doclib/partners/dro/opsmanual/visit.pdf, p. 2.

[232] GAO, *Alien Detention Standards: Telephone Access Problems Were Pervasive at Detention Facilities; Other Deficiencies Did Not Show a Pattern of Noncompliance* (July 2007) available at http://www.gao.gov/new.items/d07875.pdf, p. 10.

[233] Id., p. 15.

[234] Michele Pistone, "Justice Delayed is Justice Denied."

[235] GAO, *Alien Detention Standards: Telephone Access* (July 2007), p. 16.

[236] USCIRF, *Asylum Seekers in Expedited Removal,* Vol. II, p. 198.

[237] Correspondence between representative from Florida Immigrant Advocacy Center and Human Rights First (Aug. 2008).

[238] *Gomez-Zuluaga v. AG of the United States,* 527 F.3d 330, 339 (3rd Cir. 2008).

[239] DHS, "DHS Announces $12.4 Billion for Border Security & Immigration Enforcement" (Jan. 31, 2008).

[240] ICE, "Fact Sheet: Fiscal Year 2009" (Oct. 23, 2008), *available at* http://www.ice.gov/doclib/pi/news/factsheets/2009budgetfactsheet.doc. *See also* Nina Bernstein, "City of Immigrants Fills Jail Cells With Its Own," *New York Times* (Dec. 26, 2008).

[241] ICE, "Fact sheet: Mortality Rates at ICE Detention Facilities" (May 2008).

[242] Testimony of James T. Hayes, Jr., Director, Office of Detention and Removal Operations, "Hearing on Health Services for Detainees in ICE Custody," before the House Appropriations Committee Subcommittee on Homeland Security (March 3, 2009).

[243] See explanation in endnote 2.

[244] ICE has provided statistical information on the detention of asylum seekers in the form of reports to Congress pursuant to the Haitian Refugee and Immigration Fairness Act. In these reports, ICE only provides limited data on the length of detention for asylum seekers (until 2004, it provided an overall average length of detention, but ICE did not provide this figure in its 2006 report). These reports appear to include information only on those asylum seekers who were initially detained during the fiscal year being reported on. Therefore, the length of detention of asylum seekers detained in previous years and who continue to be detained during the fiscal year that is the basis of the report are not calculated. Similarly, the full length of detention for asylum seekers who are initially detained during the fiscal year but who remain in detention at the time the report is produced, is also not included.

[245] Calculation based on 9,971 asylum seekers detained for an average length of 93.8 days (based on statistics provided in ICE, *Report to Congress: Detained Asylum Seekers Fiscal Year 2007* (2008)), at an average daily cost of $95.

[246] Conversation between Andrew Strait, Acting Coordinator/Policy Analyst, National Community Outreach Program, ICE, and Human Rights First (March 2009).

[247] ICE, *Report to Congress: Detained Asylum Seekers Fiscal Year 2006* (2007).

[248] ICE, *Report to Congress: Detained Asylum Seekers Fiscal Year 2004* (2005).

[249] ICE, "Intergovernmental service agreement for housing federal detainees" (July 16, 2003) *available at* http://www.aclum.org/ice/documents/suffolk_contract.pdf.

[250] Cost of detention when facility first opened in 2000. Leslie Berestein, "Detention Dollars: Tougher Immigration Laws Turn the Ailing Private Prison Sector Into a Revenue Maker," *The San Diego Union-Tribune* (May 4, 2008), *available at* http://www.signonsandiego.com/uniontrib/20080504/news_lz1b4dollars.html.

[251] Josh White and Nick Miroff, "The Profit of Detention," *Washington Post* (Oct. 5, 2008).

[252] Conversation between Andrew Strait, Acting Coordinator/Policy Analyst, National Community Outreach Program, ICE, and Human Rights First (March 2009).

[253] Id.

[254] "Intergovernmental Service Agreement between the U.S. Department of Homeland Security, U.S. Immigration and Customs Enforcement, Office of Detention and Removal and Yuba County CA" available at http://www.co.yuba.ca.us/Departments/BOS/documents/agendas/2008/MG61421/AS61427/AS61430/AS61450/AI62572/DO62575/DO_62575.PDF.

[255] Cost of detention calculated at $89.50 per day. Cost of alternatives to detention program calculated at average of $10 to $14 a day.

[256] Leslie Berestein, "Detention Dollars."

[257] Cost of detention calculated at $119.28 per day. Cost of alternatives to detention program calculated at average of $10 to $14 a day.

[258] Cost of detention calculated at $82 per day. Anna Gorman, "Cities and Counties Rely on U.S. Immigrant Detention Fees," Los Angeles Times (March 17, 2009), available at http://www.latimes.com/news/local/la-me-immigjail17-2009mar17,0,764607.story.

[259] Cost of alternatives to detention program calculated at average of $10 to $14 a day.

[260] Cost of detention calculated at $161.42 per day. Cost of alternatives to detention program calculated at average of $10 to $14 a day.

[261] Cost of detention calculated at $84.51 per day. Cost of alternatives to detention program calculated at average of $10 to $14 a day.

[262] Responses of Julie Myers to Senator Edward Kennedy's follow-up Questions on the Nomination of Julie Myers to be Assistant Secretary of ICE (Oct. 23, 2007).

[263] Two weeks detention calculated based on average cost of $95 a day.

[264] The cost of detaining an asylum seeker for 3 months at the average daily cost of $95 is approximately $8,550. The cost of supervising an asylum seeker released into an alternatives to detention program for 6 months is approximately $1,800 to $2,520. Thus, even if the case lasts twice as long for an asylum seeker who is released, there would still be substantial cost savings as compared to detention.

[265] Vera Institute of Justice, Testing Community Supervision for the INS: An Evaluation of the Appearance Assistance Program Vol. I (Aug. 2000), p. 2.

[266] See, e.g. GAO, "Alien Detention Standards: Observations on the Adherence to ICE's Medical Standards in Detention Facilities," GAO-08-869T (June 2008); Dana Priest and Amy Goldstein, Washington Post, May 11, 2008; Nina Bernstein, "Few Details on Immigrants Who Die in Custody," New York Times (May 5, 2008); Department of Homeland Security, Office of Inspector General, Treatment of Immigration Detainees Housed at Immigration and Customs Enforcement Facilities," December 2006.

[267] Information on openings available at: Department of Homeland Security Division of Immigration Health Services, "Job Listings", (2009), available at https://jobs-dihs.icims.com/jobs/search?ss=1&searchKeyword=&searchLocation=&searchCategory=&searchRadius=5&searchZip=. Vacancy rate from testimony of Julie L. Myers, ICE Assistant Secretary, "Hearing on Problems with Immigration Detainee Medical Care" (June 4, 2008).

[268] Dana Priest and Amy Goldstein, "Suicides Point to Gaps in Treatment" (May 13, 2008), which reports on the case of a Somali woman detained at the Elizabeth Detention Center who was incorrectly diagnosed with psychosis without the use of an interpreter; see also Testimony of "Asfaw," before House Judiciary Subcommittee on Immigration, Citizenship, Refugees, Border Security and International Law, "Hearing on Problems with Immigration Detainee Medical Care," (June 4, 2008) (refugee from Ethiopia who was given the wring medication without the use of an interpreter).

[269] Testimony of Dora Schriro, before House Appropriations Committee Subcommittee on Homeland Security, "Hearing on Medical Care and Treatment of Immigration Detainees and Deaths in DRO Custody" (March 3, 2009); see also Dana Priest and Amy Goldstein, "Suicides Point to Gaps in Treatment" (May 13, 2008).

[270] GAO, "Alien Detention Standards: Observations on the Adherence to ICE's Medical Standards in Detention Facilities," GAO-08-869T (June 2008). See also DHS Office of Inspector General, "Immigration and Customs Enforcement's Trackign and Transfers of Detainees," OIG 09-41 (March 2009).

[271] Dana Priest and Amy Goldstein, "System of Neglect" (May 11, 2008) (reports that in January 2008, the Pearsall detention center had a backlog of 2,057 appointments).

[272] DHS, "DHS Announces $12.4 Billion for Border Security & Immigration Enforcement" (Jan. 31, 2008).

[273] Testimony of Julie L. Myers, Assistant Secretary of U.S. Immigration and Customs Enforcement (ICE), "Hearing on Problems with Immigration Detainee Medical Care" (June 4, 2008).

[274] DHS, "ICE Policies Related to Detainee deaths and the Oversight," OIG-08-52 (June 2008).

[275] Dana Priest and Amy Goldstein, "System of neglect" (May 11, 2008).

[276] Testimony of Julie L. Myers, Assistant Secretary of U.S. Immigration and Customs Enforcement (ICE), "Hearing on Problems with Immigration Detainee Medical Care" (June 4, 2008).

[277] *See* Department of Homeland Security Division of Immigration Health Services, "Job Listings", (2009), available at https://jobs-dihs.icims.com/jobs/search?pr=1 (last visited March 31, 2009).

[278] ICE, "Detention Operations Manual INS Detention Standard: Medical Care" (Sept. 20, 2000), part D; The new Performance Based Standards, effective in 2010, have a similar provision (*see* Operations Manual ICE Performance Based National Detention Standards, ICE/DRO Detention Standard "Medical Standard," Expected outcome 37 (Dec. 2, 2008)).

[279] Physicians for Human Rights, *From Persecution to Prison* (June 2003).

[280] During a visit by Human Rights First to Hampton Roads Regional Jail (November 2008), facility officials indicated they rely on guards to interpret during medical meetings; *see also* Florida Immigrant Advocacy Center, "Dying for Decent Care: Bad Medicine in Immigration Custody" (March 2009), p. 47, reporting that a nurse at the Wakulla County Jail in Florida stated she asked an ICE officer to interpret for Spanish-speaking detainees.

[281] Testimony of Ann Schofield Baker, Pro Bono Attorney for Amina Mudey, McKool Smith, "Hearing on Problems with Immigration Detainee Medical Care," before House Judiciary Committee's Subcommittee on Immigration, Citizenship, Refugees, Border Security and International Law (June 4, 2008).

[282] Dana Priest and Amy Goldstein, "Suicides Point to Gaps in Treatment" (May 13, 2008); Video: Amina Mudey's story, available at http://www.washingtonpost.com/wp-srv/nation/specials/immigration/index.html.

[283] Dana Priest and Amy Goldstein, "Suicides Point to Gaps in Treatment" (May 13, 2008); *See also* testimony of Ann Schofield Baker, "Hearing on Problems with Immigration Detainee Medical Care" (June 4, 2008).

[284] Testimony of Dora Schriro, "Hearing on Medical Care and Treatment of Immigration Detainees and Deaths in DRO Custody" (March 3, 2009).

[285] ICE, "Mortality Rates at ICE Detention Facilities" (July 17, 2008), *available at* http://www.ice.gov/pi/news/factsheets/detention_facilities_mortality_rates.htm. Fiscal year 2008 numbers current as of July 8, 2008.

[286] ICE, "Mortality Rates at Detention Facilities" (July 17, 2008); *See also* testimony of James T. Hayes, Director of Office of Detention and Removal Operations, ICE, "Hearing on Medical Care and Treatment of Immigration Detainees and Deaths in DRO Custody", before House Appropriations Committee, Subcommittee on Homeland Security (March 3, 2009) stating that "mortality rates at ICE facilities have significantly decreased since 2004" and that the "mortality rate for ICE detainees in 2008 was 2.7 deaths per 100,000 detainees. *See also* Julie Myers, "Caring for immigration detainees," *Washington Post* (May 20, 2008) *available at* http://www.washingtonpost.com/wp-dyn/content/article/2008/05/19/AR2008051902296.html.

[287] Statement of Homer Venters, MD, "Hearing on Problems with Immigration Detainee Medical Care," before the House Judiciary Subcommittee on Immigration, Citizenship, Refugees, Border Security, and International Law (June 4, 2008).

[288] GAO, *DHS: Organizational Structure* (Feb. 23, 2009), p.19.

[289] Testimony of Julie L. Myers, "Hearing on Problems with Immigration Detainee Medical Care" (June 4, 2008).

[290] Testimony of James T. Hayes, Jr., "Hearing on Health Services for Detainees in ICE Custody" (March 3, 2009).

[291] Physicians for Human Rights, *From Persecution to Prison* (June 2003).

[292] *See, e.g.,* Florida Immigrant Advocacy Center, Dying for Decent Care: Bad Medicine in Immigration Custody (Feb. 2009); Human Rights Watch, Detained and Dismissed: Women's Struggles to Obtain Health Care in United States Immigration Detention (Feb. 2009); Amnesty International, Jailed Without Justice (March 2009); Physicians for Human Rights and The Bellevue/NYU Program for Survivors of Torture, From Persecution to Prison: The Health Consequences of Detention for Asylum Seekers (June 2003), p. 64, 78.

[293] ICE, "Washington Post Detainee Health Care Series Day 3: Myths vs. Facts regarding the May 13, 2008, article," *available at* http://www.ice.gov/pi/wash_post_myth_fact3.htm.

[294] The cost of detention at the Willacy Detention Center in Raymondville, Texas, for example, is $78 per detainee per night (Spencer Hsu and Sylvia Moreno, "Border Policy's Success Strains Resources: Tent city in Texas Among Holding Sites Drawing Criticism," *Washington Post* (Feb. 2, 2007), *available at* http://www.washingtonpost.com/wp-dyn/content/article/2007/02/01/AR2007020102238.html). This is $17 cheaper than the average cost of $95 a night.

[295] See information in chapter on video conferencing in immigration court and asylum offices for credible fear interviews, and the expenses of travel costs.

[296] DHS OIG, "ICE Policies Related to Detainee Deaths" (June 2008).

[297] Vera Institute of Justice, *LOP: Evaluation and Performance Report* (May 2008), p. 63. ("LOP participants who received more intensive services had I-589 grant rates of 9.4 percent versus 2.4 percent for those LOP participants who attended group orientations alone.")

[298] See section on "Access to Legal Representation" below.

[299] Vera Institute of Justice, *LOP: Evaluation and Performance Report* (May 2008), p. iv.

[300] In 2007, ICE detained 311,169 individuals, see Office of Immigration Statistics, *Annual Report: Immigration Enforcement Actions 2007* (Dec. 2008), available at http://www.dhs.gov/xlibrary/assets/statistics/publications/enforcement_ar_07.pdf.

[301] Testimony of James T. Hayes, Jr., "Hearing on Health Services for Detainees in ICE Custody" (March 3, 2009).

[302] Vera Institute of Justice, "Legal Orientation Program" available at http://www.vera.org/cij/lop.html

[303] Correspondence between representative from Vera Institute of Justice and Human Rights First (Apr. 2009). Calculation based on estimate that LOPs will reach approximately 48,000 detained individuals out of the expected 442,941 detainees during the year.

[304] Conversation between Management Training Corporation the private corporation that manages the Willacy Detention Center, and Human Rights First (March 2009).

[305] Associated Press, "Immigration Officials Pull 600 Detainees from N.M. Jail Because of Safety Concerns," *The Arizona Daily Star* (Sept. 13, 2007), available at http://www.azstarnet.com/sn/news/201042.php.

[306] Correspondence between representative from Catholic Charities of Austin and Human Rights First (Feb. 2009).

[307] Ramji-Nogales, Schoenholtz and Schrag, *Refugee Roulette* (2007).

[308] Id., p. 340.

[309] GAO, *U.S. Asylum System: Significant Variation Existed in Asylum Outcomes Across Immigration Courts and Judges*, GAO-08-940 (Sept. 2008), p. 30.

[310] 37 percent of detained asylum seekers did not have representation in 2008, whereas 83 percent of non-detained and released asylum seekers secure representation. Statistics for fiscal year 2008 on representation for detained and non-detained asylum seekers were provided in correspondence from the Executive Office of Immigration Review to Human Rights First (Feb. 25, 2009). *See also,* Donald Kerwin, "Charitable Legal Programs for Immigrants" (June 2004). Kerwin obtained statistics from EOIR on rates of representation for fiscal year 2003. The data showed that 1,845 out of 5,537 (or 33.3%) of detained asylum and Convention Against Torture cases were unrepresented.

[311] Interviews with local pro bono legal representatives (May 2008); correspondence between a representative from Catholic Charities of Austin and Human Rights First (Feb. 2009).

[312] USCIRF, *Asylum Seekers in Expedited Removal*, Vol. II, p. 240.

[313] Vera Institute of Justice, *LOP: Evaluation and Performance Report* (May 2008), p. 24.

[314] Conversation between Jay Sparks, Assistant Field Office Director, and Human Rights First during its visit of the South Texas Detention Center, Pearsall, Texas, (May 2008).

[315] Rusu v. INS, 296 F.3d 316, 323 (4th Cir. 2002).

[313] EOIR, "Fact Sheet: EOIR's Video Conferencing Initiative" (Sept. 21, 2004).

[317] GAO, *Executive Office for Immigration Review: Caseload Performance Reporting Needs Improvement*, GAO-06-771 (Aug. 2006), p. 18.

[318] Correspondence between EOIR and the Legal Assistance Foundation of Metropolitan Chicago (March 3, 2005), included as Appendix B in The Legal Assistance Foundation of Metropolitan Chicago and Chicago Appleseed Fund for Justice, *Videoconferencing in Removal Hearings: A Case Study of the Chicago Immigration Court* (Chicago: The Legal Assistance Foundation of Metropolitan Chicago and Chicago Appleseed Fund for Justice, August 2, 2005)

[319] Jennifer Ludden, "Debate over Video in Immigration Courts," *National Public Radio* (Feb. 10, 2009), available at http://www.npr.org/templates/story/story.php?storyId=100534850.

[320] 2,723 credible fear interviews conducted by video from the Houston asylum office, out of 4,420 total credible fear interviews conducted in 2007. Information provided by USCIS, Asylum Office liaison meeting (June 17, 2008 and March 9, 2009). Information on "pass rate" for video and in-person credible fears also provided by USCIS Asylum Office.

[321] USCIRF, *Asylum Seekers in Expedited Removal*, p. 168. This rate is calculated as number of cases in which credible fear was found out of all credible fear decisions made (for 2008, credible fear was found in 3,128 cases out of 5,290 decisions made). Information provided by USCIS Asylum Office.

[322] The Houston Asylum Office has jurisdiction over Arkansas, Colorado, Louisiana, Mississippi, Oklahoma, New Mexico, Tennessee, Texas, Utah and Wyoming. *See* USCIS, "USCIS Service and Office Locator" available at https://egov.uscis.gov/crisgwi/go?action=offices.detail&office=ZHN&OfficeLocator.office_type=ZSY&OfficeLocator.statecode=OK.

[323] Credible fear interview statistics are provided by the Asylum Office on a quarterly basis during national liaison meetings.

[324] Information provided by USCIS, at Asylum Office Headquarters liaison meeting (March 9, 2009).

[325] EOIR, "EOIR's Video Conferencing Initiative."

[326] See, e.g. Sandra Hernandez, "Immigration Reforms Result in Fewer Judges, More Prosecutors," *Los Angeles Daily Journal* (Aug. 27, 2008); Spencer S. Hsu and Carrie Johnson, "Effort on Immigration Courts Faulted," *Washington Post* (Sept. 8, 2008); TRAC Immigration, "Improving the Immigration Courts: Effort to Hire More Judges Falls Short," available at http://trac.syr.edu/immigration/reports/189/.

[327] Executive Office for Immigration Review, Office of the Chief Immigration Judge, "Videoconferencing in Removal Proceedings" (Aug. 31, 2005).

[328] Frank M. Walsh and Edward M. Walsh, *Effective Processing or Assembly-Line Justice? The Use of Teleconferencing in Asylum Removal Hearings*, 22 Geo. Immigr. L.J. 259, 271 (2008).

[329] Anne Bowen Poulin, *Criminal Justice and Videoconferencing Technology: The Remote Defendant*, 78 Tul. L. Rev. 1089 (2004).

[330] U.S.C. 1229a(c)(4)(C), INA § 240(c)(4)(C).

[331] Frank M. Walsh and Edward M. Walsh, *Effective Processing or Assembly-Line Justice? The Use of Teleconferencing in Asylum Removal Hearings*, 22 Geo. Immigr. L.J. 259, 271 (2008).

[332] Rusu v. INS, 296 F.3d 316, 323 (4th Cir. 2002) ("video conferencing may render it difficult for a factfinder in adjudicating proceedings to make credibility determinations and to gauge demeanor.") See also, the Legal Assistance Foundation of Metropolitan Chicago and Chicago Appleseed Fund for Justice, *Videoconferencing in Removal Hearings*, p. 17-18.

[333] UNHCR, *Alternatives to Detention of Asylum Seekers and Refugees*, POLAS/2006/03 (April 2006).

[334] ICE Fact Sheet: Alternatives to Detention (March 16, 2009), *available at* http://www.ice.gov/pi/news/factsheets/080115alternativestodetention.htm. *See also*, Vera Institute of Justice, *Testing Community Supervision for the INS: An Evaluation of the Appearance Assistance Program*, Volume 1 (Aug. 2000), Esther Ebrahimian, "The Ullin 22: Shelters and Legal Service Providers Offer Viable Alternatives to Detention," *Detention Watch Network News*, (Aug./Sept. 2000).

[335] Responses of Julie Myers to Senator Edward Kennedy's follow-up Questions on the Nomination of Julie Myers to be Assistant Secretary of ICE (Oct. 23, 2007).

[336] Fudning for alternatives to detention: Fiscal Year 2005: $20.7 million out of $1.2 billion detention and removal budget (ICE, "Fact Sheet: Fiscal Year 2005" (Feb. 5, 2006)); Fiscal Year 2006: $38 million out of $1.6 billion detention and removal budget (ICE, "Fact Sheet: Fiscal Year 2006" (Feb. 5, 2006)); Fiscal Year 2007: $43.6 million out of $1.98 billion detention and removal budget (ICE, "Fact Sheet: Fiscal Year 2007" (Feb. 5, 2006)); Fiscal Year 2008: $53.8 million out of $2.38 billion detention and removal budget (ICE, "Fact Sheet: Fiscal Year 2008" (Dec. 28, 2007)); Fiscal Year 2009: $63 million out of $2.48 billion detention and removal budget (ICE, "Fact Sheet: Fiscal Year 2009" (Oct. 23, 2008)).

[337] Vera Institute of Justice, *Testing Community Supervision for the INS: An Evaluation of the Appearance Assistance Program*, Volume I (Aug. 2000), p. 2.

[338] Vera Institute of Justice, *Testing Community Supervision for the INS*, at iii, 8, 27, 31; Christopher Stone, "Supervised Release as an Alternative to Detention in Removal Proceedings: Some Promising Results of a Demonstration Project," *Georgetown Immigration Law Journal* (Spring 2000), p. 283, 285.

[339] Esther Ebrahimian, "The Ullin 22: Shelters and Legal Service Providers Offer Viable Alternatives to Detention," *Detention Watch Network News*, August/September 2000, at #8.

[340] *See* House Judiciary Committee Report, H.Rpt. 108-10, (report accompanying H.J. Res. 2, Omnibus Appropriations Bill of 2003), p. 626. Certain members of Congress were concerned that funds allocated for alternatives to detention were instead being used to build new detention centers. *See* Letter from Senator Leahy, Senator Hatch, Senator Kennedy and Senator Brownback to Attorney General Ashcroft, August 16, 2002.

[341] ICE, Fact Sheet: Fiscal Year 2009 Budget (Oct. 23, 2008) *available at* http://www.ice.gov/doclib/pi/news/factsheets/2009budgetfactsheet.doc; Consolidated Security, Disaster Assistance, and Continuing Appropriations Act, 2009, Committee Print of the House Committee on Appropriations on H.R. 2638 / Public Law 110-329, available at http://www.gpoaccess.gov/congress/house/appropriations/09conappro.html.

[342] ICE, Fact Sheet: Fiscal Year 2009 Budget.

[343] Responses of Julie Myers to Senator Edward Kennedy's Questions on the Nomination of Julie Myers to be Assistant Secretary, Immigration and Customs Enforcement, Department of Homeland Security (Oct. 3, 2007) ("In general, the following aliens may be considered for ATd: aliens who are not subject to mandatory detention or who have been ordered released by the appropriate judicial authority; aliens who are not deemed to be threats to the public or flight risks; and aliens who have infrastructure in place to support various electronic monitoring technologies.")

[344] Responses of Julie Myers to the U.S. Senate Committee on Homeland Security and Government Affairs, Pre-hearing Questionnaire for the Nomination of Julie Myers to be Assistant Secretary, Department of Homeland Security (Sept. 2007).

[345] Responses of Julie Myers to Senator Edward Kennedy's Questions on the Nomination of Julie Myers to be Assistant Secretary, Immigration and Customs Enforcement, Department of Homeland Security (Oct. 3, 2007).

[346] Responses of Julie Myers to Senator Edward Kennedy's follow-up Questions on the Nomination of Julie Myers to be Assistant Secretary of ICE (Oct. 23, 2007).

[347] G4S website at http://www.g4s.com/home.htm.

[348] These sub-offices are Charlotte, North Carolina; Hartford, Connecticut; and Orlando, Florida. ICE Fact Sheet: Alternatives to Detention (March 16, 2009), available at http://www.ice.gov/pi/news/factsheets/080115alternativestodetention.htm.

[349] DHS/ICE Salaries and Expenses, Program Performance Justification to Congress for FY 2009, p. 39.

[350] Responses of Julie Myers to Senator Edward Kennedy's follow-up Questions on the Nomination of Julie Myers to be Assistant Secretary of ICE (Oct. 23, 2007).

[351] ICE, Fact Sheet: Alternatives to Detention.

[352] Id.

[353] See, e.g. Megan Mack, American Bar Association, "Health Care for Immigration Detainees:
What Should Be The Standard?" (Feb. 13, 2009) (explaining that alternatives to detention programs are now being used to monitor individuals that in the past would not have been detained to begin with); Anne Sovcik Lutheran Immigration and Refugee Service, Briefing Materials Submitted to the Inter-American Human Rights Commission, Alternatives to Detention in the U.S. Immigration Detention System: Recommendations of reforms necessary to improve U.S. compliance with constitutional and international standards of procedural and substantive due process (July 7, 2008) (providing case examples of situations in which alternatives to detention programs have been used to "widen the net").

[354] Correspondence between representative from Advocates for Human Rights and Human Rights First (March 2009).

[355] Phone interview with representative from Florida Immigrant Advocacy Center (March 2, 2009).

[356] Correspondence between representative from Advocates for Human Rights and Human Rights First (March 2009).

[357] Testimony of Julie Myers, Assistant Secretary of ICE, Confirmation Hearing, U.S. Senate Committee on Homeland Security and Government Affairs Pre-hearing Questionnaire (July 26, 2007).

[358] These provisions are located primarily at 8 C.F.R. § 1003.19 and § 212.5, as well as § 208.30 and § 235.3.

[359] See, e.g., Florida Immigrant Advocacy Center, Dying for Decent Care: Bad Medicine in Immigration Custody (Feb. 2009); Human Rights Watch, Detained and Dismissed: Women's Struggles to Obtain Health Care in United States Immigration Detention (Feb. 2009); Amnesty International, Jailed Without Justice (March 2009); Physicians for Human Rights and The Bellevue/NYU Program for Survivors of Torture, From Persecution to Prison: The Health Consequences of Detention for Asylum Seekers (June 2003).

[360] http://www.dhs.gov/xnews/releases/press_release_0794.shtm

[361] GEO Group, http://www.thegeogroupinc.com/northamerica.asp?fid=107.

[362] http://www.ice.gov/doclib/partners/dro/opsmanual/visit.pdf

[363] In 2002, the former INS used 20,662 jail-like detention beds (21,262 beds minus 600 beds at the non-jail-like Broward Transitional Center facility). Department of Justice, "Fiscal Year 2000 Performance Report and Fiscal Year 2002 Performance Plan: Strategic Goal Five." This number grew to 33,400 immigration detention beds in 2009. James T. Hayes, Jr., Director, Office of Detention and Removal Operations, "Health Services for Detainees in U.S. Immigrations and Customs Enforcement Custody," before the House Appropriations Committee, Subcommittee on Homeland Security (March 3, 2009). 2,723 out of 4,420 credible fear interviews conducted by video in 2007 – all from the Houston asylum office. Information provided by USCIS, at Asylum Office Headquarters liaison meeting (June 17, 2008 and March 9 2009). Frank M. Walsh and Edward M. Walsh, Effective Processing or Assembly-Line Justice? The Use of Teleconferencing in Asylum Removal Hearings. 22 Geo. Immigr. L.J. 259, 271 (2008).

[364] Dana Priest and Amy Goldstein, "System of Neglect: As Tighter Immigration Policies Strain Federal Agencies, The Detainees in Their Care Often Pay at Heavy Cost," Washington Post, May 11, 2008, available at http://www.washingtonpost.com/wp-srv/nation/specials/immigration/cwc_d1p2.htm (accessed March 24, 2009).

[365] USCIRF, Asylum Seekers in Expedited Removal, Vol. II, p. 332

www.ingramcontent.com/pod-product-compliance
Lightning Source LLC
Chambersburg PA
CBHW051415200326
41520CB00023B/7249